5 Proven Practices to Unleash Your Passion for Teaching

HIGH FIVE

to

THRIVE

Donita Grissom PhD

Viki Kelchner PhD

Debbie Simões MEd

ISBN paperback 978-1-965438-08-4
ISBN ebook 978-1-965438-09-1

Library of Congress Control Number: 2025909648

Published by Soro Publishing
For more information about our books and authors, visit our website:
www.soropublishing.com.

This book is produced by Best Questers, a professional development organization committed to enhancing lives in practical, meaningful, and transformative ways. This resource provides a pathway for exceptional teachers to thrive and foster in an ecosystem where all students thrive and high achievement is an everyday reality.

Praise for *High Five to Thrive*

"In this love letter and thank-you note to teachers, you will find the encouragement and support you need to bring your best self to the classroom each day. Reading *High Five to Thrive* is like talking with a wise friend. Playful and fun in tone, *High Five to Thrive* offers actionable, snack-sized tips based on the authors' substantive knowledge of proven self-care practices that make us better at what we do. So, do yourself a favor and take the first step in professional self care—read *High Five to Thrive* and get started with a new way of finding fulfillment in your calling as a teacher who makes a difference!"

—Dr. Joyce Nutta, Professor, Retired from University of Central Florida

"After 30 years in education, I've read countless books and attended more in-services than I can count—but *High Five to Thrive* truly stands out. Its five practices—Purpose, Hope, Mindset, Mind-Body Harmony, and Connection—offer a powerful guide for staying energized and inspired in this profession. Whether you're a veteran teacher or just starting out, this book speaks to the heart of why we teach. It's one you'll want to keep on your desk, ready to uplift and refocus you whenever you need it."

—Ellen Oldham, School Counselor and former Teacher, Calvert County Public Schools, Maryland

"*High Five to Thrive* is a powerful tool to combat educator burnout. Grounded in research and filled with practical strategies, this book empowers teachers to rekindle their passion for the vital work of teaching. It's a book that teachers will recommend to their friends."

—Dr. Jeremy Aldrich, CTE, Gifted, and World Language Programs Director, Harrisonburg City Schools, VA

"With humor, the authors describe anecdotes and strategies to help teachers reconnect with their initial joys in interacting with children. Genuine teaching and learning begin with teachers building relationships with students. This relationship-building is possible only when teachers remain connected with their self-determined goals. This straightforward content supports teachers in reconnecting to life goals within themselves. Despite educational complexities, the authors provide teachers with a framework toward maintaining an all-important proactive mindset."

—Dr. Kathleen G. Burriss, Professor Emeritus, Middle Tennessee State University

"I just finished reading *High Five to Thrive*. More than simply a new resource for the teacher's toolbox, this book saturates you with nurturing encouragement and practical help to both keep you in the educational trenches, as well as thrive there. Whether you are a seasoned pro or just venturing into the world of education, you will see yourself on every page. Finally, someone is speaking with the voice of an educator in such a way that the reader will know the authors "get me." If you ever wondered if someone cared enough about your well-being beyond your ability to write a decent lesson plan and have solid classroom management, look no further. Get a copy for yourself and several for your colleagues down the hall. You will all be glad you did."

—Dr. Max Shelnutt, High School Teacher, Contra Costa Christian Schools

"*High Five to Thrive*" *is a* must-read for any educator who is stressed, feeling hopeless, and is ready to take charge of their circumstances and move forward. The formula that Best Questors outlines focusing on Purpose, Hope, Mindset, Mind-Body Harmony, and Connections is based on research that is time tested and just makes sense. This is a book not to be read at leisure; it should be read with the intent to grow. The last thing someone should do is to read this book and then never put the principles into practice. For over 35 years, I've served as a teacher, principal, district-level administrator, and now a teacher and leadership trainer. I've witnessed countless teachers and leaders leaving the field because of a feeling of hopelessness with complete burnout. Or, even worse, I've witnessed educators who haven't had the means to leave and are sitting in classrooms, hating every minute—with students as the losers. These educators need hope and encouragement, to remember *why* they first chose to teach and to be provided with concrete strategies and exercises they can use to address specific challenges and make positive changes in their lives and the lives of their students. Whether used for individual growth, as professional development, or as a coaching tool, this book and the resources outlined will help them to revive and thrive!"

—Jeanne Ford, EdD, JFord Equips, LLC

"After reading *High Five to Thrive*, I found myself reflecting on my journey as an educator and realizing the need to realign my current reality with the passion and purpose I felt when I first entered education over 25 years ago. The book's five Practices—Purpose, Hope, Mindset, Mind-Body Harmony, and Connection—provided a meaningful framework for assessing my own experiences and growth. The accompanying rubric guided me through a process of self-reflection, from recognizing where I was struggling to rediscovering the path to thriving. The impact of teaching through COVID was profound, leaving many educators, including myself, drained and disheartened. I watched colleagues retire early or leave the profession entirely, unable to carry the immense weight any longer. I, too, have felt that weight—the loss of joy, the exhaustion, and the struggle to reclaim the enthusiasm I once had for teaching. But this book changed something in me. Completing the pre- and post-assessments allowed me to internalize the shifts we all must make—not just in our classrooms and schools, but in our minds, bodies, and souls. *High Five to Thrive* is a powerful reminder of why we chose this noble profession in the first place. It reignites the fire within, urging us to reclaim our joy, our purpose, and our commitment to shaping the future. This book will bring teachers to tears—the sadness of what we have endured, but also the joy of rediscovering our passion. *High Five to Thrive* is a true gift to educators."

—**Dr. Marta E. Escobar,** Teacher, San Benito County Office of Education

"Fellow educators and instructional coaches will deeply value the authentic, original insights in this practical guide, designed to help educators alleviate stress and rediscover joy in their calling. Written in a tone that feels like a warm, supportive conversation with a trusted colleague, this guide offers realistic strategies for protecting our passion and maintaining a sense of purpose in a profession that often feels like an uphill battle. It's a must-read for those seeking sustainable fulfillment in the challenging yet rewarding field of education."

—**Raisa Perez,** FCC Liaison and ESOL Instructional Coach, Family Connection Center, Seminole County, Florida Public Schools

"*High Five to Thrive* makes an important, practical contribution to the growing literature on teacher well-being and helping teachers thrive both inside and outside of the school setting. Their strategies vary from positive cognitive affirmations to sensory mindfulness strategies, so teachers can reflect on what works best for them, and which strategies can be incorporated in an on-going manner most easily into their lifestyles. Teacher well-being is important for all of us because it impacts student well-being and achievement. Thriving teachers have thriving students, and this book provides a very accessible tool to help teachers as human beings, so that they are best equipped to help the human beings in their classrooms."

—Dr. Sarah Bassin Burton, School Psychologist, Richland School District Two, Columbia, South Carolina

"*High Five to Thrive* is a fantastic read for any educator who wants to elevate their teaching while also taking care of themselves. The authors lay out five simple steps that help you reconnect with your core purpose—the reason you got into teaching in the first place. I love how it balances self-care with professional growth, making it clear that when teachers thrive, students benefit, too. It's a practical and inspiring guide that's definitely worth checking out if you want to make a real impact in the classroom without burning out. Highly recommended!"

—Françoise Vandenplas, Supervisor of World Languages for Montgomery County, MD, Public Schools

"I've been in education for 20 years, and *High Five to Thrive* truly spoke to me. It helped me step back and face not just the burnout, but the deep hurt and trauma I carry every day. I'm still in a place where any negative experience brings that pain right back. This book reminded me that the teacher I once was, the one I still want to be, is not lost. But I still question whether healing is worth the mental toll it takes. Rebuilding trust feels nearly impossible when I have to stay guarded just to get through the day. What I appreciated most is that this book does not pressure you to fix everything. It gives you space to be honest, to start where you are, and to protect your peace. I never thought anyone would take the time to speak to the deep wounds educators carry. I am truly grateful for this book and the authors who had the heart to write it."

—Jamie White Lexington, Kentucky

Dedication

First of all, I have to dedicate this book to all of the "bumps in the road," times of waiting, hindrances, frustrations, failures, heartaches, losses and lessons learned in all of them! While this sounds strange, these things have shaped who I am and have given me treasures of wisdom to share. My hope is that these golden nuggets will save you from having to experience some of these things I endured. It is also my hope that you will be able to shape your own path through the wisdom you glean all along the way. I hope you will write new stories from flipping your scripts. Next, I have to dedicate this book to my two Hope Agents who have worked with me furiously to write this book. We have so many stories to share, and I hope that the pages of this book will continue to grow as we go and meet some of you along our journeys out in the field. I thank my family for putting up with my ideas and creative processes. I love them with everything in me! I thank God for allowing me to carry this purpose in my heart and share it with all of you!

Spreading hope and joy,

Donita

Donita Grissom, PhD

This book is dedicated to all the teachers who show up every day for their students, even on the toughest days—those who dig deep, push through, and find the strength to inspire, even when the weight of the world feels heavy. Your resilience, dedication, and passion do not go unnoticed. You are shaping lives, creating futures, and making an impact that extends far beyond the classroom.

I thank God for the gift of life and for bringing Donita, Debbie, and me together on this incredible journey. The bond we share and the vision we hold have made this work possible, and I am endlessly grateful for their wisdom, encouragement, and unwavering support. To my family, whose love remains steadfast and unconditional, thank you for being my foundation, guiding light, and greatest source of strength.

Lastly, to every educator who has walked alongside me—those who have inspired me, challenged me, mentored me, and lifted me up—I am profoundly grateful. Your encouragement, wisdom, and belief in the power of education have helped shape me into the person I am today. This book is a tribute to the work you do, the lives you touch, and the lasting impact you create. May it remind you of your purpose, renew your passion, and empower you to continue making a difference.

With much gratitude,

Viki

Viki Kelchner, PhD

To the teachers who rise each day, embracing the challenges and triumphs of shaping the future—one student at a time—this book is for you. You may not always hear the gratitude you deserve, but let this be a reminder: your efforts are seen, your encouragement changes lives, and your dedication is leaving an immeasurable impact.

Through my years as a teacher, school administrator, and leadership coach, I have witnessed the unwavering resilience, passion, and heart it takes to do what you do. Teaching is more than a profession; it is a calling, commitment, and powerful force for change.

May this book bless you with renewed energy, strengthened momentum, and fresh inspiration to transform your classroom into a place of joy, possibility, and growth. As you continue to pour into the lives of your students, I hope these words pour into you, reminding you of the incredible work you do every single day. You are shaping the world, one lesson, one moment, one student at a time.

And to Mr. Fabulous, the wind beneath my wings, thank you for being you! Your light, energy, and enthusiasm bring joy and inspiration to everyone around you—especially me.

Together we thrive,

Debbie

Debbie Simões

Contents

Praise for *High Five to Thrive*   iii

Introduction   1

Practice 1:
Purpose   19

Practice 2:
Hope   29

Practice 3:
Mindset   47

Practice 4:
Mind-Body Harmony   65

Practice 5:
Connections   83

Conclusion   105

References Cited   119

About the Authors   125

Bring High Five to Thrive into Your School or District   129

What People Are Saying   133

Introduction

To Every Educator
Who Has Ever Wondered,
"Is This Still for Me?"

Some children spent their days pretending to be astronauts or future presidents, but some of us found joy in setting up a classroom with dolls and pets as their students. With a chalkboard in hand and a well-worn Webster's dictionary, they eagerly played the role of teacher, captivated by the idea of sharing knowledge. For those with a passion for education from an early age, the dream was never about reaching the stars; it was about inspiring others to learn.

Maybe you've always felt comfortable with children or teens, and they seem to gravitate to you. At birthday parties when your friends had their younger siblings there, you loved making them laugh. Perhaps you had a teacher who inspired you and sparked that dream of making a difference, just like they did. Or maybe you come from a proud family of educators, and you felt that stirring inside to carry on the tradition.

I bet you remember the excitement of getting your first teaching job, setting up your classroom, glowing with anticipation and passion to touch each life with your heart, the heart of a teacher! You know your purpose. You have the gifts and talents! You were born for this!

Close your eyes, and let your mind take you back to the beginning of your journey as a teacher. What were you feeling? What do you remember thinking? As you reflect back, what thoughts and feelings are coming up for you now? What has changed? What has remained constant? Is being a teacher everything you dreamt it would be?

In these trying times teachers in every corner of the world are wrestling with this very question.

They're juggling challenges such as large class sizes, discipline problems, difficult parents, increasing demands, and mounting responsibilities, in addition to providing instruction, cafeteria duty, professional learning community meetings, insufficient support, inadequate resources, pressure to teach to standardized tests, endless paperwork, politics, bureaucracy, faculty meetings and professional development sessions that are not meaningful, an unhealthy school culture, feeling overwhelmed, unappreciated, undervalued, underpaid. . . and the list goes on and on. (Can you scream "AHHHHH!"?)

The Struggles Educators Face: The Research Behind the Problem

Teaching is more than a career—it's a calling. But it's also one of the most demanding, emotionally exhausting professions in the world. According to Gallup (2022), nearly 44 percent of K–12 educators report feeling burned out "always" or "very often," making teaching one of the most stressful professions in the US. Additionally, research from the National Education Association (NEA 2022) indicates that 55 percent of educators are considering leaving the profession earlier than planned due to overwhelming workloads, unsustainable expectations, and increasing emotional exhaustion. Additionally, there are 500,000 fewer educators in public schools than there were before the pandemic (Peck 2024).

Many educators feel that their salary is not commensurate with their workload, level of responsibility, or education. According to the Economic Policy Institute, in 2022, public school teachers earned an average weekly wage of $1,329, while other college graduates earned $2,167 per week. This reflects a weekly wage gap of $838, translating to an annual difference of approximately $43,576 (Economic Policy Institute 2022).

A McKinsey & Company (2022) study found that teachers work an average of 50 hours per week, nine hours more than other professionals, often at the expense of their well-being. Similarly, RAND Corporation (2021) reports that teachers are twice as likely to experience frequent job-related stress compared to other working adults. The demands of teaching can also include increased administrative tasks, lack of support, and challenging student behaviors, leading to high levels of stress and burnout. More than 80 percent of teachers report that student behavior has worsened significantly in recent years, which exacerbates their stress (Peck 2024; NEA

2022). More than 75 percent of teachers have reported experiencing stress-related health issues, highlighting the ongoing need for support and well-being initiatives (Peck 2024; NEA 2022).

On top of these challenges, many teachers cite a lack of adequate support and resources as a major factor driving them away from the profession. Without the tools and backing needed to manage their classrooms and address the diverse needs of their students, teachers are left feeling overwhelmed and undervalued (McKinsey & Company 2022).

Last but not least, the rigidity and bureaucracy of the education system can stifle creativity and professional growth. Research shows that lack of autonomy and opportunity for professional growth also led to disenchantment (McKinsey & Company 2022).

Beyond the numbers, what does this really mean? Many teachers experience an internal crisis—one that isn't just about external challenges but about how they feel inside.

Are You Experiencing Any of These?

Have you ever woken up exhausted, questioning why you chose this career? Do you find yourself drained by endless demands, struggling to find the joy in teaching that once fueled your passion? Maybe you've noticed a creeping sense of self-doubt, wondering if you're truly making an impact. Perhaps you feel disconnected—from your students, your colleagues, or even from the very purpose that brought you into education in the first place.

If any of this resonates with you, you're not alone. Many educators face the same daily challenges, and these challenges often lead to frustration, burnout, and even thoughts of leaving the profession altogether.

Loss of purpose. Is the passion that once fueled you fading? Studies show that educators with a strong sense of purpose experience lower burnout and greater job satisfaction (Ryan and Deci 2020).

Feeling of hopelessness. Have you ever felt like no matter what you do, it's not enough and you're left feeling hopeless? Recent research indicates that many teachers are experiencing profound hopelessness—persistent stress and insufficient support are key contributors to burnout and diminished well-being (Pressley 2021).

Unhelpful mindset patterns. Do you ever notice that your automatic thoughts negatively shape your view of yourself, your students, and your classroom environment? This can lead to increased stress and reduced classroom effectiveness (Jennings and Greenberg 2019).

Overlooking mind-body harmony. Do you ever feel overwhelmed and stressed out? Research shows that neglecting the mind-body connection—the essential link between your thoughts, emotions, and physical well-being—can significantly contribute to chronic stress (Roeser et al. 2012).

Feeling disconnected from work, students, and colleagues. Research shows that strong teacher-student relationships are directly linked to engagement and achievement (Hamre and Pianta 2006). When you feel detached, everyone suffers—including you.

What's Bugging You?

Let's hone in on *your* list. What chips away at your job satisfaction? Take a moment to write down anything that bothers you in the What's Bugging You document in the Bonus Content.

Scan to Unlock Bonus Content (What's Bugging You?)

Pre-Assessment

This pre-assessment is designed to help you reflect on where you currently stand in key areas that impact your well-being and effectiveness as an educator. The bar graph will help you visualize your strengths and areas for growth across five practices, which we hone in on in this book.

Scan to Unlock Bonus Content (Pre-Assessment)

Steps to Complete the Assessment

1 **Read each question carefully.** Take a moment to reflect on each question and how you feel about it.

2 **Assign a rating.** For each question, choose the rating that best reflects your feelings or experience. Use the scale below:

1 = Not at all

2 = Somewhat

3 = A good amount

4 = Extremely so

3 **Calculate your average rating.** Each category has two related questions. Add your two ratings together for each category and divide the total by 2 to find your average rating for that area.

High Five to Thrive Pre-Assessment

Record your rating for each question.

Purpose – Feeling connected to your "why"	
How clear is your sense of purpose and meaning in your work as an educator?	Rating
Do you have defined goals for the impact you want to make in your students' lives?	Rating
Average rating	

Hope – A thriving mindset and belief in possibilities	
How hopeful and optimistic do you feel about your future in education?	Rating
When challenges arise, how often do you feel confident in your ability to stay solution-focused and resilient?	Rating
Average rating	

Mindset – The thoughts and self-talk that shape your self-belief and how you handle life

How often is your internal dialogue positive and encouraging?	Rating
Do you actively try to shift negative self-talk to a more supportive mindset?	Rating
Average rating	

Mind-Body Harmony – Prioritizing well-being without guilt

How often do you engage in self-care practices that support your mental and physical well-being?	Rating
Do you feel in control (or not in control) of your emotional and physical well-ness, especially in stressful situations?	Rating
Average rating	

Connections – Building relationships that uplift and sustain you

How strong are your relationships with your students?	Rating
How connected do you feel to a supportive community of educators?	Rating
Average rating	

Plot your results. Take your average rating for each category and mark it on the scoring rubric.

Pre-Assessment Scores by Strategy

4

3

2

1

0

Purpose (Q1 & Q2)   Hope (Q3 & Q4)   Mindset (Q5 & Q6)   Mind-Body Harmony (Q7 & Q8)   Connections (Q9 & Q10)

High Five to Thrive Pre- and Post- Assessment Scoring Rubric

This is the rubric with clear descriptors for each of the five practices, scored on a 1–4 scale, to guide reflection and progress.

Practices	1-Beginning	2-Exploring	3-Developing	4-Thriving
Purpose Feeling connected to your "why"	Is completely disconnected from purpose. Lacks motivation and passion.	Has moments of passion and engagement but lacks consistency.	Regularly connects with purpose and finds meaning in teaching.	Fully embodies and lives their purpose daily, inspiring and leading others.
Hope A thriving mindset and belief in possibilities	Feels stuck and overwhelmed by problems. Struggles to see possibilities. Primarily focuses on obstacles and lacks confidence in overcoming them	Is beginning to reframe challenges into opportunities and explore solutions. Takes small steps toward positive problem-solving but still experiences self-doubt.	Uses hopeful thinking to navigate difficulties and actively looks for solutions. Demonstrates resilience and begins to apply tools to shift focus from obstacles to opportunities.	Naturally turns obstacles into opportunities and thrives in uncertainty. Fully embraces a growth mindset, confidently taking action to create solutions and inspire hope in others.
Mindset The thoughts and self-talk that shape your self-belief and how you handle life	Negative self-talk dominates, leading to self-doubt and discouragement. Struggles to recognize or challenge negative thoughts.	Uses some positive self-talk tools but inconsistently. Has moments of confidence but still struggles with self-doubt in challenging situations.	Applies positive self-talk regularly to boost confidence and resilience. Actively works to reframe negative thoughts and maintain a balanced mindset.	Mastery of self-talk, with automatic positive thought patterns that uplift and empower. Inspires and mentors others in developing a resilient and confident mindset.

Practices	1-Beginning	2-Exploring	3-Developing	4-Thriving
Mind-Body Harmony Prioritizing well-being without guilt	Experiences extreme stress, exhaustion, and burnout. No self-care or well-being tools in place, leading to emotional and physical strain.	Implements some stress management techniques but inconsistently. Begins to prioritize self-care but still experiences frequent burnout.	Engages in self-care and stress regulation with reasonable consistency. Has tools in place to maintain energy and manage emotions.	Fully integrates well-being into daily life, effortlessly balancing stress and energy. Thrives in a state of calm, focus, and resilience, inspiring others to do the same.
Connections Building relationships that uplift and sustain you	Feels isolated and disconnected from colleagues, students, or the school community. Avoids collaboration and struggles to engage in meaningful interactions.	Actively working on building relationships and collaboration. Finds value in connecting with others but still struggles with consistency or depth.	Builds and maintains meaningful connections with colleagues and students. Engages in collaboration and communication regularly, fostering a positive environment.	Thrives in a network of deep, lasting, and positive connections that uplift all. Acts as a connector, fostering a strong sense of community and belonging.

Rating Interpretation

✍ 5–8: **Beginning:** Your journey is just beginning. This book will guide you in developing the tools to help you become the best version of yourself!

✍ 9–12: **Exploring:** You have some pieces in place. Focus on refining your approach to strengthen your impact and satisfaction.

✍ 13–16: **Developing:** You're well on your way! Keep applying these tools to thrive in your teaching and well-being.

✍ 17–20: **Thriving:** You are thriving! Add new or strengthen your practices to sustain growth and inspire others.

Reflect on the Results

If your response was less than a 4 on any or even all of these questions, don't be dismayed! Or, if your ratings were lower than 2 on most or all of your questions, remember, this is a baseline for you at this moment. Know that you are not alone, and we have good news for you! Hope is on the way! Wherever you are in your journey as an educator, if you believe your classroom or school is destined for distinction, and you feel a stirring in your heart, then you're right and you're in the right place!

These struggles don't only affect teachers; they affect students, school culture, and the broader educational system. What if you could shift the way you experience teaching? What if you could reconnect with your purpose, cultivate hope, and create a more sustainable, fulfilling career?

Use the tools in this book to enhance your well-being in areas where your ratings are lower.

The Solution: The Best Questers High Five to Thrive Formula™

If you've ever found yourself driving to work wondering "Can I do this for another year?" If you feel like you're giving everything but have nothing left for yourself, or if you're searching for a way to reignite your passion for teaching, this book is for you.

This book doesn't focus on what's broken in education. It focuses on what's within your control: your purpose, hope, mindset, mind-body harmony, and connections. The Best Questers High Five to Thrive Formula™ is a proven, action-driven formula that helps you move from frustration to fulfillment, burnout to balance, and hopelessness to hope.

Thriving isn't about just surviving another school year; it's about rekindling the fire that made you want to teach in the first place. It is the process of growing, thriving, and living with purpose, and fulfillment. It means feeling energized, resilient, and confident as you navigate challenges while experiencing joy, hope, success, and personal growth.

Whether you are a veteran teacher or brand new, this formula is your roadmap to maximizing joy and impact in your profession. Each of the five practices provides tool(s) that can help you reclaim your passion and thrive in your career.

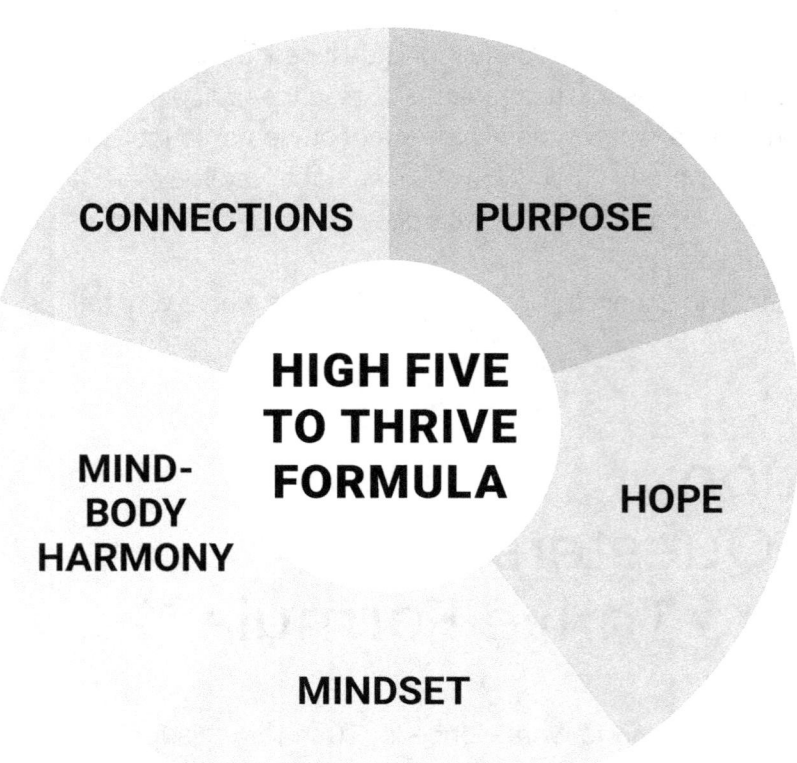

Practice 1: Purpose – *Feeling connected to your "why"*

Your passion for education is still there; you just need to uncover it again. This practice helps you rediscover your purpose, clarify your "why," and create a vision that keeps you motivated, even in the face of challenges.

Practice 2: Hope – *A thriving mindset and belief in possibilities*

Hope isn't just a feeling; it's a strategy. Research shows that hope is a predictor of resilience, motivation, and success. This practice enables you to develop and sustain a hopeful mindset that carries you through obstacles and inspires your students.

Practice 3: Mindset – *The thoughts and self-talk that shape your self-belief and how you handle life*

Your inner dialogue shapes your reality. Negative self-talk can drain your energy, confidence, and relationships. This practice focuses on mastering your mindset, replacing self-doubt with empowering beliefs, and building the mental resilience needed to thrive.

Practice 4: Mind-Body Harmony – *Prioritizing well-being without guilt*

Educators often put themselves last, but the truth is you cannot give your best to others if you are running on empty. This practice helps you integrate practical, sustainable self-care tools into your routine, so you can show up as your best self every day.

Practice 5: Connections – *Building relationships that uplift and sustain you*

Teaching is not meant to be a solo journey. Meaningful relationships—with students, colleagues, and administrators—are key to thriving in education. This chapter helps you build stronger connections that support your success and well-being.

Self-Care Isn't a Luxury

If you are still here with us, we are so glad to see you are not one of the national statistics described in this book! Your role in shaping brighter futures is vital, and we believe in your ability to keep making an extraordinary impact, even when the road feels tough.

Let's be honest: some of the factors that limit your satisfaction are outside of your control, such as your pay, your schedule, and testing mandates. I wish we could erase all of those challenges, but unfortunately our eraser isn't that big. So, we are going to focus on what we do have control over, starting with the most obvious: ourselves. Maybe you're thinking, "I have too much to do to waste time on a book or workshop about self-care and wellness!" I hear you. But, without you– *a fully present, wholesome, healthy, happy you*– what do you have to give to your students???

This is why we need to stop, focus on you first, and then you'll be better equipped with strength and vitality to accomplish everything you are required to do and actually enjoy your job. You'll be amazed at how quickly you'll see results by making just one or two small pivots, results that transform how you and your students experience school. We call these "small biggies" because they are small tweaks that make a big impact.

Stephen Covey, renowned author of *The 7 Habits of Highly Effective People*, wisely said, "If I really want to improve my situation, I can work on the one thing over which I have control—myself." We are excited to be on this journey with you and help you discover just how powerful you are because you matter. Your self-care is not a luxury; it is a daily must-have to tap into your teaching superpowers every day.

We All Have a Story

Think back to the early days of *your* story, when you were a child in school. Who were the main characters that shaped your story? If you think about it, at that stage of your life those main characters were actually writing much of your story, weren't they?

Here is a story from one of our authors, Debbie Simões:

"When I was in fourth grade, our jolly old principal retired and was replaced by the formidable Sister Victoire. Until then my school story was a happy one with gold stars and singing. In the chapter Sister Victoire co-wrote, I pretended to be sick and hid in the closet when it was time to leave for school. Finally, my mom dragged me in and had a talk with Sister Victoire. I watched from the other side of the venetian blinds in the waiting area, hot tears burning my cheeks and a knot in my stomach. I remember the terror I felt when my mom came out and escorted me into the principal's office. Sister Victoire spoke to me in what I imagine was her kindest voice, but I heard nothing. Then, through the blinds, I saw my mom getting into her car. 'Nooooo!' Frantically, I ran out of the school, through the parking lot, onto the road and all the way down the hill. Thank God the light at the bottom of the hill was red, and I caught up to the car! My mom had that look on her face that every kid dreads: a mix of shock and fury. Unfortunately, she took me back to school. At the end of the day my teacher told her I had cried all day, and after that my parents found another school for me.

I wonder if Sister Victoire had any idea of her influence on that chapter of my story. I wonder if *we* have any idea of the impact we have on the children and families we serve. Generally speaking, people tend to have very little awareness of their impact on others, good or bad. As teachers, we are a primary author of each student's story, and of a collective story as well. The stories we're writing matter! These stories have lifelong implications for each and every character in them."

You Matter!

That's why it's so important that we are mindful of our own well-being and our influence. We have to guard our passion and sense of purpose. We must intentionally grow in ways that empower us to write impactful stories that set ourselves and our students on a path of becoming the best possible versions of ourselves and also create a sense of "we" in our schools.

We're all in this together! Protecting your enthusiasm and leaning into your purpose can create an experience for you and your students that catapults you to a higher level in terms of who you are and, most importantly, the lifelong impact you have on the students you serve. You're the architect of your classroom culture, and you can create a safe space where you and your students love stepping into your greatness together each day.

Everything begins with you...with your awareness, your well-being, your vision, your action steps, and stepping into your power! The Best Questers team is excited to support you on your quest to excel as an educator and love every minute of it, as you should! It is an honor to offer you this formula to thrive and close the gap between your hopes and dreams as a teacher, and your everyday reality. In case you haven't heard this today, we will be reminding you: you matter!

How This Book Is Structured

Each of the five practices is intentionally structured around the Best Questers High Five to Thrive Formula™, so you don't just read about thriving—you gain the practices to experience it.
Every practice is detailed in the following path:

WHAT: Know the Problem

+ Define the core problem or struggle.

+ Gain clarity on what is holding you back.

+ Recognize how this challenge impacts your growth.

HOW: Learn a Tool for Thriving

+ Gain a practical tool or framework to overcome obstacles.

+ Break the solution into actionable, manageable steps.

+ Read examples of how to integrate this practice into your life.

WHY: Understand the Importance

+ Explore why this practice matters in your transformation.

+ Identify limiting beliefs that may be holding you back.

+ Reframe your mindset to fully embrace the shift

+ Realize the choice is yours.

SCIENCE BEHIND THE STRATEGY: Research for Practical Impact

+ Understand the research to apply proven methods that improve engagement, retention, and success.

+ Know the science to advocate for, communicate, and make informed decisions.

+ Use proven practices to teach with confidence, effectiveness, and well-being.

MEET THE TEACHER: See Real-Life Applications

+ Read inspired realistic stories based on our experiences and those of our colleagues.

+ Understand how teachers just like you navigated challenges and thrived.

+ Find inspiration in their journey to help fuel your own.

A TEACHER'S MEMOIR: Learn from Others

+ Gain insights from research and real-world applications.

+ Explore different perspectives on implementing this practice.

+ Learn how small shifts lead to significant outcomes.

+ Discover powerful moments from a teacher's memoir

YOUR TURN: Take Action for Traction

+ Apply the concept to your own life through guided exercises.

+ Set a personal goal or challenge related to the practice.

+ Track your progress and measure small successes.

JOURNALING: Reflect and Bloom

Journaling is important for several reasons:

+ **Reduces stress and enhances clarity.** Writing helps process emotions, lower anxiety, and organize thoughts.

+ **Boosts problem-solving and self-awareness.** Reflecting on challenges fosters solutions, emotional intelligence, and personal growth.

+ **Encourages positivity and motivation.** Tracking progress, documenting wins, and setting goals build optimism and accountability.

+ **Supports mindfulness and creativity.** Journaling promotes self-care, gratitude, and creative expression.

+ **Strengthens memory and learning.** Writing reinforces knowledge and serves as a personal archive of growth and lessons learned.

Here are tips to journal effectively:

+ **Start small and stay consistent.** Set aside just five minutes a day, and establish a routine that works for you.

+ **Use prompts and reflection.** Spark ideas with guided prompts, express thoughts freely, and explore challenges to find solutions.

+ **Practice gratitude and affirmations.** List things you're grateful for, and write empowering statements to boost positivity.

+ **Visualize and track progress.** Describe your ideal future, and revisit past entries to see your growth.

+ **Make it your own.** Personalize your journal with creative elements such as drawings, bullet points, or storytelling.

COACHING QUESTIONS: Sustain Growth

+ Write down questions you still have about the content, yourself, feelings, emotions, etc.

+ Questions can be used for discussion with a small group, in a book study, or with a friend.

+ You can email Best Questers at info@bestquesters.net with your questions at any time.

+ Coaching Conversations – If you are part of a professional learning community (PLC) or working with a mentor, these questions can facilitate productive discussions and support.

Each practice is designed to take you from recognition to resolution, allowing you to experience sustainable growth and hope-powered thriving. By the end of each chapter, you will have gained insights, a concrete plan, and the confidence to take action for traction.

The Path to Thriving Starts Here: Commitment

Before we dive in, take a moment to honestly reflect on how open you are to learning some simple, practical and potentially life-changing tools to experience *less stress and more smiles*. The potential of these tools to improve your life and your students' lives is directly related to your openness to receive and try out new ideas. Are you ready to step out of your comfort zone and step into the legacy in which you were born to thrive, not strive? Empowerment is just one step outside of your comfort zone. We invite you to go *all in* on this adventure.

Write out your commitment in your own words in the space below using the present tense (not future tense). The Best Questers community is *for* you, and we'll keep your tank filled with hope, which is the high-octane fuel that will empower you to drive transformation in your classroom.

Scan to Upload Bonus Content (Sample Commitment Statement)

Sample Commitment Statement *I'm ready to learn some simple, practical, and life-changing practices to reduce stress and find more joy. I'm open to new ideas and willing to step out of my comfort zone. I'm ALL IN for this adventure and excited to transform my classroom with the support of the Best Questers community. Let's do this!*

The Power of Small Biggies

Some of the ideas and suggestions in this book may be familiar, and some will be new to you. Some might present a challenge. The magic is in how these practices weave together to create a new paradigm rooted in connecting with and honoring yourself, your calling, and others.

Remember in the story of *The Three Little Pigs* that the house that withstood the wolf's fierce huffing and puffing was the one made of brick? You'll find a beautiful array of bricks in this book, but the magic is not in the bricks. It's the way we *arrange* the bricks and the *mortar* we use to bind them together that can help you build a structure that will stand the test of time.

We invite you to be on the lookout for small biggies—those small changes that deliver big results. As you read and reflect, zero in on small shifts you can make that will have the biggest impact on how you feel about yourself, your students and your job, how you "show up" at school, and how you can create a more joyful and empowering school experience for yourself and your students. Remember: small biggies!

By the time you finish this book, you will have tools to help you do the following:

+ **Tune into your purpose** and why you became a teacher in the first place.

+ **Learn how to flip the script** on your mindset, self-doubt, and negative thoughts.

+ **Strengthen resilience** by developing small but powerful habits that create lasting change.

+ **Find new ways to connect** with students and colleagues to make your work more meaningful.

+ **Take action** in ways that bring joy, balance, and impact back into your teaching.

This transformation won't happen overnight, but with small, intentional steps, you'll begin to see real, lasting change. Teaching is a journey, and you're about to take a powerful step forward.

Are you ready to thrive? Let's begin.

Practice 1: Purpose

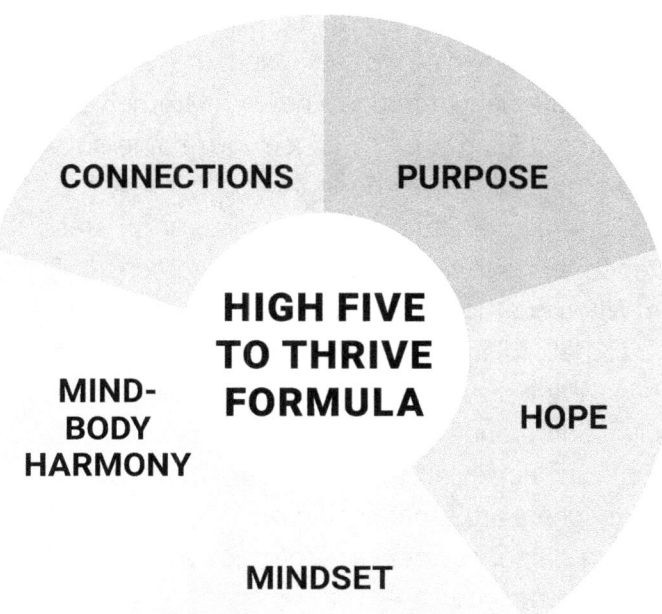

CONNECTIONS

PURPOSE

HIGH FIVE TO THRIVE FORMULA

MIND-BODY HARMONY

HOPE

MINDSET

WHAT: Know the Problem

Many people think teachers are in the business of education working with children and young people, but they have it backward. As teachers, we are in the business of children and young people, working on their education. Our business is children and young people, not education. We get off course when we lose sight of this.

Missiles have a guidance system that makes course corrections to ensure the intended target is hit. In education, standardized testing is our "guidance system" that guides our course corrections. We go to great lengths and create enormous pressure to hit our target, which we call the standards. But does this system reflect a focus on children or on education? Similarly, looking at it from another level, does our system focus on teachers or on instruction? The challenges we are facing today suggest that we have lost sight of our intended target: people. We are in the business of children and young people, supporting their education. We accomplish this by being in the business of teachers, supporting their instruction.

Imagine if our schools adopted the ideal that John Maxwell instills in his team of 40,000 wildly successful leadership coaches: "We are people of value who value people and add value to them." Let's break that down so we can absorb the full measure of power and wisdom in this simple statement. It forges a powerful framework for a life well-lived because it encapsulates valuing yourself (since you're a person, too), valuing others (all others), and the piece not everybody thinks of...making a practice of adding value to yourself and others. If we adopt this as our north star, it becomes the context of our existence and cultivates a vibrant shared sense of community, altruism, and excellence. When our thoughts and actions align with this simple but profound ideal, it sets us on a path to success and significance, two core values nearly every teacher holds dear. We believe significance is a driving force for teachers—that deep desire to make a difference in the lives of children and the equally deep satisfaction that comes from achieving that purpose. Yet, research shows that this is not the reality most teachers are experiencing.

Do you feel like you are sliding down a slippery slope? Or worse, has your dream job turned into a nightmare, like an awful dream you can't wake up from?

This is what it feels like to be disenfranchised or disconnected from your purpose. It's a bitter pang of disappointment, like a cherished dream turning to dust in your hands. The spark that ignited your passion for teaching feels dimmed, replaced by the dull ache of disillusionment.

Here are warning signs you may be disconnected from your purpose:

+ You feel burned out and exhausted.

+ You question your impact or whether what you do even matters.

+ You're going through the motions, lacking motivation and joy.

+ You feel like you've lost control over what happens in your classroom.

+ You feel more like a manager than a mentor.

If you are a seasoned teacher, then imagine the excitement you once felt at the prospect of nurturing young minds, sharing knowledge, and seeing the "light bulb moments" of understanding in your students' eyes. Does that enthusiasm feel distant, replaced by a sense of frustration or even cynicism? The challenges of the job, the feeling of being undervalued, or a mismatch between the idealized image and the reality may have chipped away at your inspiration. It can be a confusing state of limbo. You question whether this is just a temporary feeling or a sign that you need a change. There's a lingering fondness for the dream you once held, tinged with the sadness of letting it go.

It's like mourning the loss of a potential future you once envisioned for yourself. You may have forgotten your value or feel like you have nothing of value to give. (New teachers, keep reading! We equip both new *and* experienced teachers with ways to journey through these real issues and feelings. Remember, your passion to teach is a superpower, and Best Questers is here to strengthen you along the way no matter where you currently are.) Our goal is to help you reconnect with the deep sense of purpose, passion, joy, hope, and meaning that brought you to teaching in the first place.

HOW:
Learn a Tool for Thriving

One way to overcome feeling disenfranchised or disconnected from your dream due to negative circumstances is to take a few minutes to write about what initially drew you to your job and the aspects you once loved. This is like giving your brain a mini-vacation and a shot of optimism. It's a simple yet powerful tool to help you bounce back and approach your challenges with a renewed sense of connection to your work.

Action for Traction Step:
Purpose Reflection Exercise

Take five minutes to write about the following:

+ **Why** did you become a teacher?

+ **What** was a defining moment in your career that made you feel like you were making a difference?

+ **Add examples** of how happy you felt when a student of yours let you know how much you had changed their life; or a moment when you saw your students really get what you were teaching and how good that made you feel.

+ **When** was the last time you felt truly fulfilled in your role?

Keep these best practices in mind:

+ Keep this reflection positive! Focus on the moments that sparked your joy and deepened your purpose.

+ Keep your reflection. This is something you can read when you're having a "dream-not-so-true" day.

WHY:
Understand the Importance

When you write about what you love about your job and keep it somewhere visible, it serves as a powerful reminder during stressful moments. Reading this statement about your calling helps shift your focus and mood, keeping negativity in check. When stress kicks in, the brain naturally leans toward negative thinking, but revisiting what you enjoy about your work gives your brain a positive focus—similar to gratitude journaling, which is known to improve mood.

The note you place on your refrigerator, the post-it on your desk, or even a statement set as your laptop screensaver becomes a physical cue. Just glancing at it during a stressful moment can help restore balance, reducing stress through attention restoration. Writing things down also frees up mental space, allowing you to offload stress from your working memory. Fostering gratitude in this way has been linked to stress reduction and increased well-being—exactly what we're aiming for, right?

Focusing on the positive aspects of your job shifts your mindset from frustration to appreciation. This simple shift activates the brain's reward centers, releasing dopamine, a feel-good chemical that improves mood and reduces stress. Seeing the bigger picture helps you recognize challenges as temporary bumps in the road rather than insurmountable obstacles, leading to greater resilience.

Finally, reminding yourself of what you find fulfilling about your work can reignite your passion and sense of purpose. This renewed spark of motivation can help you tackle difficult tasks with energy and confidence. The best part? This technique requires little effort and can be easily repeated throughout the week to reinforce your stress-reduction practices. You can even apply this strategy to other stressful areas in life. Writing things down makes it even more effective, as it engages more areas of your brain than simply thinking about it, creating a tangible record you can revisit when you need it most.

Below are some benefits of writing down your "why":

+ Shifts focus from stress to positivity.

+ Creates a physical cue that restores balance.

+ Frees up mental space and reduces cognitive overload.

+ Activates the brain's reward system, improving mood and reducing stress.

+ Strengthens resilience by helping you see challenges as temporary.

+ Reignites passion and motivation for your work.

+ Provides a simple, repeatable stress-reduction strategy.

+ Engages more areas of the brain, reinforcing positive thinking.

Taking a few seconds to reflect on your "why" can help you stay grounded, energized, and connected to what truly matters. So, what's your "why?" Write it down and let it work its magic!

SCIENCE BEHIND THE STRATEGY: Research for Practical Impact

+ **Shifting focus reduces stress.** Reading a reminder of what you love about your job helps shift focus and improve mood, similar to gratitude journaling, which has been shown to boost happiness and reduce stress (Sparby 2018).

+ **Physical cues help reset your mind.** Seeing a positive note on your desk, fridge, or screensaver works as an attention reset, refocusing your brain and reducing mental fatigue (Yap et al. 2022).

- **Dopamine boost improves mood and resilience.** Thinking about what you enjoy at work activates dopamine, the brain's "feel-good" chemical, helping to reduce stress and increase motivation (Schultz 2015).

- **Gratitude and positive reframing build emotional strength.** Practicing gratitude and focusing on positive aspects of work can reframe challenges as temporary setbacks instead of overwhelming obstacles, which fosters resilience and emotional well-being (Li et al. 2022).

- **A simple, repeatable habit fosters long-term benefits.** Writing down and revisiting what you love about your job trains your brain to stay positive, reduces stress, and helps you feel more engaged over time. This small habit creates a lasting impact on motivation, well-being, and overall job satisfaction (Barton et al. 2023; Emmons, et al. 2023).

How To Use This Daily: Post this reflection somewhere visible: on your desk, as a phone screensaver, or in your planner. Just glancing at it can reignite your passion in tough moments.

MEET THE TEACHER:
See Real-Life Application

From the time she was a young girl, Ms.Carter dreamed of being a teacher, inspiring students with her love of learning. She envisioned creating a nurturing environment where children could thrive, discovering the joy of knowledge and the satisfaction of mastering new skills. For years, she felt like she was living her dream, but lately, the increasing pressure of standardized testing was zapping and draining all the energy and enthusiasm from her fifth-grade classroom.

She was spending more and more time teaching to the test, drilling facts and figures into her students' heads rather than fostering a genuine love for learning. She felt like she was losing sight of her true purpose: to be in the business of children, supporting their education in a holistic and meaningful way. One afternoon, after a particularly grueling day of test preparation, Ms. Carter sat alone in her classroom. The walls, once covered with colorful artwork and inspiring quotes, now bore charts and graphs tracking students' progress toward meeting state standards. The desks, which used to be arranged in collaborative groups, were now lined up in rows to simulate the testing environment. She stared at the data on her computer screen, feeling a heavy weight on her chest. She began to cry and feel hopeless. "What am I going to do?" she wondered.

A TEACHER'S MEMOIR: Learn from Others

Today, I took five minutes to reflect on why I became a teacher. In the middle of lesson planning, grading, and back-to-back meetings, I paused to write down the moments that truly matter. Instantly, my mind shifted from stress to gratitude.

I thought about Natasha's heartfelt letter—the one where she thanked me for believing in her, even when she struggled. The stress that had been weighing on me suddenly felt lighter, replaced by a rush of warmth and energy. It was as if my brain hit a reset button, reminding me why this work is so important.

Then, I remembered Juan's breakthrough moment—when he finally shouted, "I get it now!" after wrestling with a math problem. That memory alone reminded me that my efforts matter. Taking time to write it all down not only helped me process these emotions but also gave me a much-needed boost of motivation.

Now, I keep this reflection on my desk and as my phone's screensaver. Just glancing at it in a tough moment helps me shift my mindset, breaking the cycle of stress and reconnecting me to my purpose. It's a small habit, but it makes a big difference.

Instead of letting burnout take over, I've found a simple way to bring myself back to the moments that make teaching worth it. And the best part? I can do it anytime, anywhere—just five minutes of writing, a quick glance at my note, and I'm reminded of the joy in what I do.

Highlights of Ms. Carter's Experience

Ms. Carter experienced a profound transformation through the reflective exercise that reignited her passion for teaching. Below are the highlights of her journey, along with how each impact aligns with scientific research:

+ **Shifting focus to reduce stress.** Ms. Carter set aside five minutes to reflect on the meaningful moments in her teaching career. Amidst the pressures of planning, grading, and meetings, she found that writing about these experiences helped her shift from stress to gratitude. Just like gratitude journaling, this small habit boosted her happiness and lowered her stress levels (Sparby 2018).

- ✦ **Using physical cues to reset the mind.** To keep her motivation strong, Ms. Carter placed a written reflection on her desk and saved it as her phone's screensaver. Whenever stress crept in, a quick glance at these reminders helped her refocus and regain clarity, reducing mental fatigue throughout the day (Yap et al. 2022).

- ✦ **Boosting mood and resilience with dopamine.** Recalling moments like a heartfelt thank-you note from Natasha or Juan's triumphant "I get it now!" in math class triggered Ms. Carter's brain's reward system. These reflections activated dopamine, the brain's natural feel-good chemical, reinforcing her motivation and reducing stress (Schultz 2015).

- ✦ **Reframing challenges through gratitude.** Writing down her experiences helped Ms. Carter see setbacks as temporary rather than overwhelming. By focusing on the positive, she strengthened her resilience and emotional well-being, enabling her to navigate challenges with a more optimistic outlook (Li et al. 2022).

- ✦ **Creating a habit for long-term benefits.** By consistently revisiting what she loves about teaching, Ms. Carter trained her brain to stay positive. This simple, repeatable habit not only reduced her stress but also increased her job satisfaction, motivation, and overall well-being over time (Barton et al. 2023; Emmons et al. 2023).

Each step of her reflective journey not only transformed her outlook but also provided her with a scientifically backed tool for reducing stress, boosting well-being, and strengthening her resolve as an educator.

YOUR TURN:
Take Action for Traction

Scan to Unlock Bonus Content (Your Turn- Take Action for Traction)

Take five minutes to write about why you became a teacher. Add examples of how happy you felt when a student let you know how much you had changed their life, or describe a moment when you saw your students really get what you were teaching and how good that made you feel. Keep this piece of writing positive and full of the wonderful things you love about being a teacher. Keep this! It's something to revive you when you are having a "dream not so true" day.

Unlock this strategy and even more powerful strategies and exclusive resources at BestQuesters.net, where you thrive and grow with purpose and impact.

JOURNALING:
Reflect and Bloom

Scan to Unlock Bonus Content (Journaling- Reflect and Bloom)

REMEMBER, this page is for you to write down your feelings, struggles, successes, anything you feel you need or want to process after reading this chapter. If you are not accustomed to journaling, you can:

1. **Start with a prompt.** If you're unsure where to begin, you can use these guided prompts:

   » How has your sense of purpose in education evolved since the beginning of this journey?

   » What specific experiences or insights have helped you clarify the impact you want to make in your students' lives?

» If your purpose feels stronger or clearer now, what contributed to that shift? If it still feels uncertain, what might help solidify it further?

2. **Write freely and honestly.** Don't worry about grammar or structure. This is your space to express yourself openly.

3. **Make it your own.** Customize your journaling practice with doodles, pictures, bullet points, creative storytelling, or any format that helps you reflect and connect with your journey.

Take a deep breath, let your thoughts flow, and allow this space to support your growth and transformation.

COACHING QUESTIONS:
Sustain Growth

As a reminder:

Scan to Unlock Bonus Content (Coaching Questions-Sustain Growth)

+ **Write** down questions you still have about the content, yourself, your feelings, emotions, etc.

+ **Discuss** questions in small groups, in a book study, or with a friend.

+ **Email** Best Questers with your questions at any time (info@bestquesters.net).

+ **Discuss** in coaching conversations in professional learning communities or working with a mentor to facilitate productive discussions and support.

Practice 2:
Hope

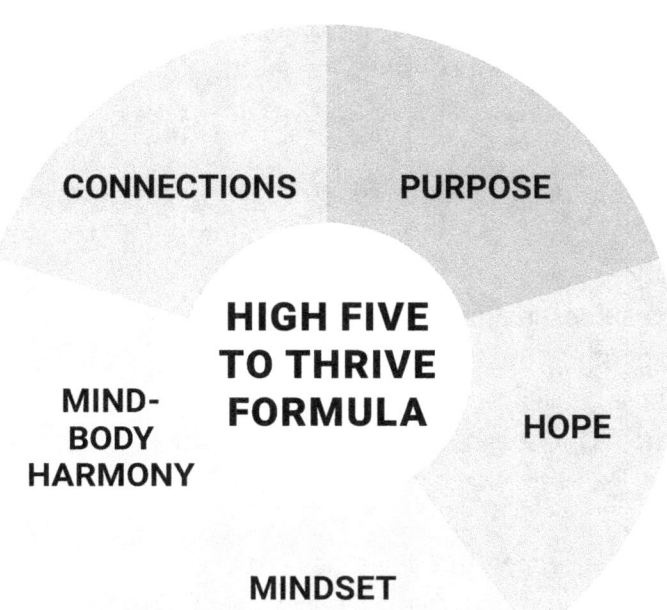

CONNECTIONS

PURPOSE

HIGH FIVE
TO THRIVE
FORMULA

MIND-
BODY
HARMONY

HOPE

MINDSET

WHAT:
Know the Problem

Do you ever feel like you're stuck in a rut? Like life's just throwing problems at you left and right? Yeah, we do, too. But here's the thing: those problems are like that glass of water, right? Think about it. You see it as half empty, bummed out there's not more. What if you flip the script? Suddenly, it's half-full, not bad at all! It's all about perception.

We can choose how we see things. Sure, there will always be stuff that's not ideal, bumps in the road. But instead of getting stuck on the "empty" feeling, why not grab that "full" feeling and run with it? We want to help you turn your problems into actionable goals. Those problems may be the exact fuel you need to get moving toward some pretty awesome goals.

Have you ever gone mountain climbing? Taking on a big challenge is a lot like climbing a mountain. To reach the top (your goal or solution to your problem), you need three things. First, you need a clear view of the peak. In other words, what exactly is it you are trying to achieve? What is it you're working toward? Maybe it is something necessary or maybe something exciting that motivates you to climb. It can be big or small, but it should be crystal clear in your mind. If you are not sure what you are needing or wanting, you may run out of energy to get there. If you aren't clear on what you are trying to solve, when the climbing gets rough, you may be tempted to stop.

When you see the top, you are more determined to keep climbing, no matter what. That's what it's like to really know what your goal is, or making the solution to that problem the very goal you want to obtain.

Once you've established your peak destination, it's time to map out your ascent. There's seldom a single, direct path to the top. Instead, multiple routes wind their way upward, each offering unique challenges and rewards. Perhaps one path is steep and demanding, while another is gradual but scenic. The flexibility to adapt your approach is essential. Obstacles, like unexpected weather conditions or unforeseen barriers, are inevitable.

Having alternative paths prepared can mean the difference between reaching your summit and being forced to retreat. In other words, it's always good to map out multiple paths up the mountain. Having options means you can adjust your plan in the face of hindrances or hurdles. These are called your pathways. They are the "how."

Finally, and perhaps most importantly, you must believe in your ability to make it to the top. Confidence is the mental strength of mind that propels you forward when the climb becomes difficult. It's the inner voice that reminds you of your capabilities and encourages you to persevere. When doubt creeps in, it's this belief that anchors you, preventing you from giving up. Remember, every seasoned climber will attest to the fact that the journey is as rewarding as the destination. The belief that you can endure that climb is your agency, your confidence in yourself. It's the willpower, hope-filled thoughts and motivation factor that keeps you going when the climb gets harder. A good climber believes they can navigate the challenges and reach the summit. This is the part of hope that the inner critic interferes with. We will deal with that hope-hacker later in this chapter.

Hope is all about having these three things working together. You need a goal to keep you motivated, a plan to get you there, and the belief in yourself to see it through. With all three on board, you're well on your way to conquering your mountain (or whatever your goal or problem solution may be). Hope is your reminder that brighter days are ahead, but it's up to you to make it happen. Stay focused, take action, and keep moving forward—one step at a time—to turn that hope into reality.

HOW:
Learn a Tool for Thriving

We will use the Hope Action Plan to work on turning our problems into workable, actionable goals. Let's explore the parts of the Hope Action Plan:

Goal or problem. Start by clearly writing down the issue you're facing. Be specific. The more precise you are, the easier it is to craft a targeted goal. You can use the SMART Goals framework to help you create crystal clear goals:

✦ **Specific:** Be very clear about what you want to achieve.

✦ **Measurable:** Establish a way to track your progress. How will you know you're getting closer to your goal?

✦ **Attainable:** Set a goal that is challenging but achievable within your capabilities and resources.

✦ **Relevant:** Be sure your goal aligns with your overall objectives and desires.

✦ **Time-bound:** Set a deadline for achieving your goal. This creates a sense of urgency and keeps you focused. Remember, this is a repetitive process. As you work toward your goal, you might need to refine it based on new information or changing circumstances.

Visualize and describe. Visualize and describe your desired outcome. You can close your eyes and imagine the ideal scenario where the goal is reached or the problem is solved. What would things look like? How would you feel? Visualizing success provides a clear picture of what you're working toward. Write it down so you can look at it when you are having one of those "not-so-dream-come-true days" that we talked about in Chapter 1.

Strategies. Brainstorm ways (pathways) you can work toward the goal. In other words, identify the things you will do to accomplish your mission (goal) or solve your problem.

Motivation. You may spend a lot of time here analyzing the thoughts that help or hinder you. We call those thoughts that hinder us *hope-hacking thoughts*. We all have them, but we can flip them into hope-filled thoughts that energize us and provide fuel for the journey, instead of being stuck on the side of the road. We call that *flipping the script*. So jot down those thoughts, both hope-hacking and high-hope ones. Don't be embarrassed. We will show you how to flip the script (turn those hope hacking thoughts into powerful hope-filled thoughts) in this chapter.

In this same row, think about how you will celebrate each of the steps you accomplish in your journey toward reaching the goal or solving the problem. Celebrations are incredible for the brain, which directs the body in happy ways with feel good hormones that energize us. When we celebrate, we motivate ourselves. Let's be honest: we could all use some more self-celebration.

Hope agents. If you are one of those people who say, "I don't know how," then that's a great time to ask a Hope Agent. Hope Agents are supportive people who have "been there and done that" and will take you by the hand and help you all along the way. Don't be afraid to ask. We all need help and are better off when we have support and someone to cheer us on. There is nothing wrong with leaning in to others when we need to. The hard part may be knowing when we need to lean in. Knowing what and who you have to work with helps determine the feasibility of your goal or problem solution. You can jot those names down in the Hope Agent section.

Hope habits. Once you accept the mission and put these hope tools to work for you, you'll unlock a powerful superpower: hope habits. Hope habits are intentional, repeatable actions for traction that cultivate a mindset of optimism, resilience, and forward-thinking. Just like physical habits shape our health, hope habits shape our mental and emotional well-being by reinforcing positive self-talk, problem-solving, and goal-setting.

+ **Why they matter:** Hope isn't just a feeling—it's a skill that can be strengthened through daily practice. When we engage in **hope-building behaviors consistently**, we rewire our brains to focus on **possibilities instead of limitations**.

+ **Examples of hope habits:**

» **Flipping the script** – Replacing negative thoughts with hopeful, action-oriented ones.

» **Celebrating small wins** – Acknowledging progress, no matter how small, to build momentum.

» **Visualizing success** – Mentally picturing positive outcomes to boost confidence and motivation.

» **Practicing gratitude** – Shifting focus from what's missing to what's working.

» **Engaging in solution-focused thinking** – Asking, *"What's one step I can take toward a better outcome?"*

✦ **The science of hope habits:** Repeating hopeful actions strengthens neural pathways, making hope a natural response rather than an effortful choice. Research suggests it takes 63 days to form a lasting habit (Leaf, 2021), meaning that hope can become second nature with consistent practice.

Hope isn't just something you feel—it's something you build. Start small, stay consistent, and watch your hope habits transform your mindset and your life! These hope habits will guide you to the results you're aiming for, turning your efforts into lasting, meaningful change. Therefore, in the Hope Habits section, list some ways you will start to build hope habits.

Hope stacking. Hope habits include a powerful concept called hope stacking. This is about building small, consistent habits that stack up to create a more hopeful mindset and a stronger routine. Imagine adding a hopeful thought, action, or achievement each day, and over time, watching your entire outlook transform!

How can you turn your goals into a daily practice that becomes second nature? While we may not have magic wands or genies, author James Clear's idea of habit stacking is one of the most effective tools at your disposal. Habit stacking means pairing a new behavior with an existing one, making it easier to integrate the new habit into your routine.

You might already be doing this without even realizing it. Ever place your medication next to your toothbrush so you remember to take it or set something by your keys or shoes so you don't forget it? Maybe you've kept a water bottle within reach to remind yourself to stay hydrated. You're already familiar with the concept. Now, it's about applying it with the intention to build your hope habits and create lasting change.

Could a visual reminder or an alarm on your phone help you stay on track? For example, we recently made a small change to boost our productivity at work. We each taped a sign to the top of our computer monitors that said, "Is what I'm doing right now the best use of my time?" Throughout the day, we notice the sign, and often, the answer is no. That simple reminder helps us refocus, making sure we're choosing tasks that truly move us in the direction of our goals.

What tools could you use to make sure your new hope habits stick? Here are some ideas:

✦ **Write it down.** Capture your ideas in writing as a declaration of your commitment.

✦ **Share your plan.** Tell at least one person about your Transformation Plan. You are more likely to stick to your goals when you share them with someone who supports and holds you accountable.

✦ **Create a Hope Jar.** Every time you achieve a small win (small biggie), drop a note or token into the jar. Over time, watching it fill up becomes a powerful visual reminder of your progress.

Scan to Unlock Bonus Content (Hope Jar)

✦ **Build a support group.** Find or create a group of like-minded individuals who are also working on their hope habits. Encourage each other through group messages or meet-ups, making hope stacking a collective effort. Remember your Hope Agents?

✦ **Make yourself Victory Vouchers.** Our middle names are "Fun!" We love to have fun! Celebrating successes along the way can make habit-building more sustainable. Rewards can be anything that brings joy—like a movie night, a special outing, or a small gift for yourself. The anticipation of reaching these milestones adds an element of excitement. Fill in the "Victory Vouchers" with fun ways to celebrate your small wins, such as "Dance for five minutes" or "Treat yourself to your favorite dessert." Mini-celebrations make the habit-building journey more lighthearted, and the element of surprise makes it feel like a game. By associating your habit-building process with something like the Victory Vouchers, you transform the journey into a playful, rewarding experience, making it easier to stay consistent and motivated. So in the Hope Stacking section, make a hope stacking plan of how you will help yourself build those hope habits!

Scan to Unlock Bonus Content (Victory Voucher)

Hope Action Plan Sample

GOAL or PROBLEM What am I working on?	Making time for myself every day to do something I enjoy.
VISUALIZE and DESCRIBE	I see myself feeling more balanced, energized, and fulfilled. Instead of feeling overwhelmed by daily responsibilities, I create a dedicated time each day to do something just for me—reading, walking, listening to music, or enjoying a hobby. This time helps me recharge and approach my day with more patience and positivity.
STRATEGIES How will I reach my goal or solve my problem?	Schedule 15–30 minutes daily for an activity I enjoy. Set a reminder or block time on my calendar. Start small—just 5–10 minutes if needed—and build from there. Identify activities that bring me joy and relaxation. Reduce distractions by turning off notifications or creating a quiet space.
MOTIVATION Hope-Hacking Thoughts to Change Energizing, Hope-filled Thoughts Ways to Celebrate	**Hope-Hacking Thoughts to Change** **Hope-Hacking:** I never have enough time **Hope Filled:** I deserve time for myself. **Hope-Hacking:** I always have bad days **Hope-Filled:** Even small moments of joy can improve my day. **Hope-Hacking:** I never take care of myself **Hope-Filled:** Taking care of myself helps me show up better for others. **Ways to Celebrate** ✦ Treat myself to a small reward at the end of the week. ✦ Acknowledge my progress and how it makes me feel. ✦ Share my success with a friend or support group.

HOPE AGENTS Who will you ask for help?	A close friend or family member to check in and encourage me.
	A mentor or coach to remind me of the importance of self-care.
	A community or support group with similar goals.
HOPE HABITS	Begin my day with a positive affirmation about self-care.
	Track my daily self-care activities in a journal or app.
	Pair my self-care time with another habit (e.g., after lunch or before bed).
HOPE STACKING	Listen to uplifting music while engaging in my self-care activity.
	Combine self-care with movement, such as walking outdoors.
	Use positive self-talk before and after my daily activity to reinforce the habit.

These tools not only help build habits but also create an environment that fosters continuous personal growth, which in turn can increase your hope levels, improve your overall personal wellness and your relationships with others. Integrating these into daily life or within your story's narrative will allow a hopeful mindset to become part of your identity and character.

WHY: Understand the Importance

People with high hope levels perform better at work, experience greater life satisfaction, and set and achieve more goals (Emmons and McCullough 2003). The best part? Hope isn't just something you're born with; it's something you can build.

Clear goals and problem-solving skills—the foundation of hope theory (Snyder 1991)—provide direction and purpose, fueling motivation to take action and pursue dreams. Hopeful individuals also have strong problem-solving abilities, seeing obstacles as opportunities for creative solutions and resilience rather than roadblocks. They also benefit from better cognitive functions such as memory and attention.

Hope boosts confidence and has even been linked to improved physical health and overall well-being. Research suggests that high hope can enhance immune system function, demonstrating its potential impact beyond mental health.

Hopeful individuals also tend to be more optimistic and positive, making them enjoyable to be around. This positivity helps build stronger relationships with friends, family, colleagues, and students. People with high hope levels also exhibit better communication skills, higher empathy and compassion, and lower stress and anxiety levels.

Students with higher hope levels are more engaged, earn better grades, and set and achieve more goals than their low-hope peers. In the workplace, hope fuels motivation, job satisfaction, and success.

The power of hope is clear. Thinking about these benefits may motivate you to cultivate more hope in your own life.

Benefits of High Hope Levels

- ✦ Increases motivation and goal achievement.

- ✦ Enhances problem-solving skills and resilience.

- ✦ Boosts cognitive functions such as memory and attention.

- ✦ Improves confidence, physical health, and immune function.

- ✦ Strengthens relationships and communication skills.

- ✦ Reduces stress, anxiety, and promotes emotional well-being.

- ✦ Leads to higher engagement and success in school and work.

- ✦ Fosters happiness, fulfillment, and life satisfaction.

Hope is a skill you can develop, and its impact extends into every area of life. So, why not start building yours today?

SCIENCE BEHIND THE STRATEGY: Research for Practical Impact

Having high levels of hope is like a superpower for success and well-being. Here are a few of the many reasons why:

- ✦ **Increases motivation and enhances problem-solving.** Hopeful individuals set clear goals, stay driven to take action, and persist through challenges. Instead of getting stuck in setbacks, they explore alternative solutions and new ways to move forward (Snyder 1991).

- ✦ **Boosts resilience and protects against stress and burnout.** Hope acts as a psychological buffer, helping individuals bounce back from adversity while preventing emotional exhaustion. High-hope individuals see challenges as opportunities for growth (Snyder 1991).

- ✦ **Improves mental and physical health.** Hopeful people experience less stress, better emotional regulation, and even stronger immune function. Research suggests that hope lowers stress-related illnesses, reduces inflammation, and enhances overall well-being (Fredrickson 2009; Snyder 1991).

- ✦ **Strengthens relationships and social connections.** Hopeful individuals tend to have more positive interactions, stronger communication skills, and deeper social connections, fostering meaningful relationships (Snyder 1991).

- ✦ **Higher academic and career success.** Studies show that students and professionals with high hope perform better, achieve higher grades, and reach long-term goals more effectively (Snyder 1991).

- ✦ **Enhances self-confidence and life satisfaction.** Hope strengthens the belief in one's ability to create change, take control of the future, and experience greater life satisfaction and overall happiness (Snyder 1991; Gallagher and Lopez 2009).

- ✦ **Enables the brain to "rewire" for lasting change.** When hopeful thoughts and behaviors are repeatedly practiced, they strengthen positive neural pathways, reinforcing long-term resilience and optimism. Small, repeated actions (hope habits) lead to lasting behavioral changes (Duhigg 2012).

- ✦ **Habit-stacking for sustainable hope.** Connecting new hopeful habits to existing routines makes them easier to sustain over time, reinforcing hope as a daily practice (Fogg 2019).

MEET THE TEACHER:
Real-life Application

Teaching high school wasn't quite what Mrs. Harris had envisioned. She sat, staring at the towering stack of ungraded essays, the fluorescent lights overhead humming in rhythm with the dull ache in her head. It hadn't always been like this. Once, she had thrived on the energy of creativity, captivated by the stories pouring from her students' minds. But now, each essay felt less like a window into their imagination and more like another weight pressing down on her already burdened shoulders.

Collapsing in her chair, Mrs. Harris rubbed her eyes. Exhaustion gnawed at her, a constant companion that followed her from the classroom to her empty house. The joy, the passion that had ignited her love for teaching, seemed to have dimmed to embers. "Burnout," she whispered, the word tasting bitter on her tongue.

A TEACHER'S MEMOIR:
Learn from Others

There I was, staring at the never-ending pile of papers on my desk, exhaustion pressing down on me like a weight I couldn't shake. My shoulders ached, my mind felt like mush, and my heart just wasn't in it anymore. This wasn't how teaching was supposed to feel. I wasn't meant to be a machine, mindlessly pushing through each day. I wanted more. I refused to let this be my story.

So, I grabbed a notepad and wrote down the problem: overwhelming exhaustion and a loss of joy in teaching. Seeing my thoughts in ink made them real, a stark acknowledgment of how much I had been carrying. Then, I closed my eyes and let my mind drift back to when teaching truly lit me up. I remembered the excitement of stepping into my classroom: the buzz of creativity, the shared laughter, and the deep connections with my students. That memory sparked something in me—a flicker of hope. I needed that feeling back.

I decided to take action. No more just pushing through. I set a goal: two yoga sessions a week. Something small but intentional—something that would help me recharge, rewire my brain, and build better habits. To make it happen, I came up with a plan. I kept my yoga clothes in the car, set reminders on my phone for Tuesdays and Thursdays at 4:00 pm, and promised myself a coffee date with my best friend after eight weeks to celebrate. She also agreed to check in on me, making sure I stuck with it.

Of course, doubt crept in almost immediately. What if I didn't have time? What if I quit after a week? What if this didn't work? But this time, I caught myself. I rewrote the narrative in my head: I may feel tempted to skip yoga because of grading, but if I don't take care of myself, I won't have the energy to enjoy teaching or life. If I want my joy and connection back, I must—and I will—put myself first.

The first week wasn't easy, but I did it. And then the next. And the next. Slowly, I started to feel different. My motivation grew because I had a clear goal to push toward. I realized that the days I did yoga I was more present in my classroom. I had more energy. I laughed more with my students. The stress didn't weigh me down as much. I started seeing challenges not as roadblocks but as problems I could solve. It was like my brain was learning a new way to think—more flexible, more hopeful.

Hope wasn't just something I felt anymore; it was something I practiced. The small, repeated actions were stacking up, rewiring my mind little by little. I could feel it, and the best part was, it wasn't just about yoga. It was about learning to put myself back in the equation, to recognize that I matter, too.

I keep my reflections on my desk now—a reminder of why I teach and who I am. On the hard days, I glance at them, and they reset me, pulling me back to what's important. This isn't just about self-care. It's about something deeper. It's about hope—the kind you build, the kind you fight for, the kind that transforms everything.

Highlights of Mrs. Harris' Experience

Through the Hope Action Plan exercise, Ms. Harris learned several valuable lessons that reignited her sense of purpose and determination. Here are the highlights of her journey:

Increases Motivation and Enhances Problem-Solving

+ Writing about overwhelming exhaustion and loss of joy provided clarity for Mrs. Harris, shifting the focus from feeling stuck to creating a solution.

+ As Mrs. Harris set a clear, meaningful goal—two yoga sessions per week—activated motivation and problem-solving, helping to find new ways to push through obstacles.

+ Reframing setbacks as challenges to solve made it easier to stay committed and persist.

Boosts Resilience and Protects Against Stress and Burnout

+ Establishing a structured self-care routine created **a psychological buffer** against exhaustion and burnout.

- Recognizing the need for joy and connection transformed stress into a **renewed sense of purpose** rather than a burden.

- Taking consistent hopeful actions helped **bounce back from fatigue**, preventing emotional exhaustion from taking over.

Improves Mental and Physical Health

- Yoga became a physical and emotional reset, **reducing stress and improving energy** levels.

- The structured approach to self-care led to **better emotional regulation**, helping to navigate challenges with more balance and control.

- Hopeful thinking and intentional action helped reduce feelings of anxiety and restore **a sense of well-being** in both personal and professional life.

Strengthens Relationships and Social Connections

- Increased energy and joy **deepened connections** with students and colleagues, making classroom interactions more engaging and fulfilling.

- Having an accountability partner provided **social encouragement**, reinforcing the importance of connection and mutual support in sustaining habits.

- Stronger self-care led to **more presence and patience** in relationships, enhancing personal and professional bonds.

Higher Academic and Career Success

- Increased motivation and resilience made it easier to **stay engaged in teaching**, leading to more creativity and effectiveness in the classroom.

- Prioritizing personal well-being **led to greater job satisfaction**, improving overall performance as an educator.

- The shift in mindset transformed **day-to-day challenges into opportunities for growth**, increasing long-term success.

Enhances Self-Confidence and Life Satisfaction

- Taking action to reclaim joy reinforced the belief in personal ability to **create change and regain control** (Snyder, 1991).

- Progress toward small goals **increased self-confidence**, making it easier to sustain motivation and momentum (Gallagher & Lopez, 2009).

- A daily reflection habit helped **maintain perspective and appreciation** for the work being done (Gallagher & Lopez, 2009).

Enables the Brain to "Rewire" for Lasting Change

- Repeatedly practicing hopeful actions strengthened neural pathways, making **positive thinking** and problem-solving more automatic (Duhigg, 2012).

- Each small success reinforced **a pattern of resilience and optimism**, shifting mindset from survival mode to growth (Snyder, 1991).

- Tracking progress helped **sustain motivation** by providing visible proof of improvement over time (Duhigg, 2012).

Habit-Stacking for Sustainable Hope

- Small, hopeful actions like **keeping a yoga bag in the car and setting reminders** made new habits easier to maintain (Fogg, 2019).

- Attaching hope-based actions to **existing routines (hope stacking)** created consistency, reinforcing long-term well-being (Fogg, 2019).

- The structured approach to hope turned into a **daily practice, ensuring lasting impact on energy, motivation, and fulfillment** (Fogg, 2019).

Hope is your superpower. It's not just a feeling; it's a strategy that turns problems into possibilities. By taking small, consistent steps, you can shift your mindset, take control, and create real change. Your next step starts today. Let's climb this mountain together—one step at a time.

YOUR TURN:
Take Action for Traction

Use the Hope Action Plan to map out your next goal or problem that you want to turn into an actionable goal. Be sure to keep track of your successes and celebrate! Watch your hope grow and grow because that's what hope does when it has the right conditions to help it grow.

Remember the **Hope Action Plan** includes:

+ **GOAL/PROBLEM:** What am I working on?

+ **VISUALIZE & DESCRIBE**

+ **STRATEGIES:** How will I reach my goal or solve my problem?

+ **MOTIVATION:** Hope-Hacking Thoughts to Change; Energizing, Hope-filled Thoughts; Ways to Celebrate

+ **HOPE AGENTS:** Who will you ask for help?

+ **HOPE HABITS:** intentional, repeatable actions for traction to increase hope

+ **HOPE STACKING:** small, consistent actions that stack up to create stronger hope habit

JOURNALING:
Reflect and Bloom

REMEMBER, this page is for you to write down your feelings, struggles, successes, anything you feel you need or want to process after reading this chapter. If you are not accustomed to journaling, you can:

Scan to Unlock Bonus Content (Journaling-Reflect and Bloom)

1. **Start with a prompt.** If you're unsure where to begin, you can use these guided prompts:

   » How has your level of hope about your future as an educator changed?

   » What tools have you implemented that help you stay solution-focused and resilient when challenges arise?

   » How do you plan to continue nurturing a hopeful and empowered mind-set moving forward?

2. **Write freely and honestly.** Don't worry about grammar or structure. This is your space to express yourself openly.

3. **Make it your own.** Customize your journaling practice with doodles, pictures, bullet points, creative storytelling, or any format that helps you reflect and connect with your journey.

Take a deep breath, let your thoughts flow, and allow this space to support your growth and transformation.

COACHING QUESTIONS:
Sustain Growth

Scan to Unlock Bonus Content (Coaching Questions- Sustain Growth)

As a reminder:

+ **Write** down questions you still have about the content, yourself, your feelings, emotions, etc.

+ **Discuss** questions in small groups, in a book study, or with a friend.

+ **Email** Best Questers with your questions at any time (info@ bestquesters.net).

+ **Discuss** in coaching conversations in professional learning communities or working with a mentor to facilitate productive discussions and support.

Practice 3: Mindset

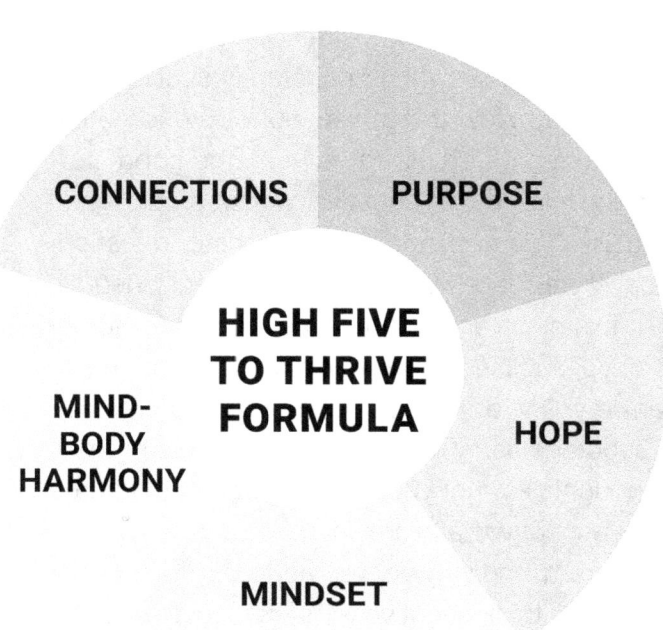

CONNECTIONS

PURPOSE

HIGH FIVE
TO THRIVE
FORMULA

MIND-
BODY
HARMONY

HOPE

MINDSET

WHAT:
Know the Problem

"I am so stupid."

"I must be the worst teacher ever!"

"I am miserable and nothing ever goes right for me!"

"My students don't like me."

"No one at the school likes me."

Have any of these thoughts run through your mind? As educators, we have all had these miserable hope-hacking thoughts. They can be relentless, constantly criticizing, belittling, judging, condemning, shaming, and questioning. They make sure you do not forget anything you ever did wrong. They try to convince you that you did things you never did. They even criticize your thoughts: "What's wrong with you thinking these kinds of thoughts? What kind of person are you? You must be crazy!"

Maybe you have heard of this phenomenon as the "inner critic." You can choose to call it whatever you want to call it. That nagging voice is determined to make you feel like a real worry-wart. It's like a super-anxious friend constantly scanning for danger, even if it's not really there. It loves to blow things way out of proportion. It turns minor setbacks into full-on disasters and forgets to mention the good stuff that happens. It also loves to play fortune teller, with a negative twist. It predicts bad intentions in others, assuming they dislike you even with no evidence or questionable evidence to support it. This edgy pest makes you expect to be punished for any mistake, like falling out of favor. It fixates on any hint of lost affection in interactions, turning them into threats. This hypervigilance, always looking for what could go wrong, can lead to long-lasting anxiety. One of their favorite phrases is "what if."

These voices in our mind try to sabotage us by getting us to grab hold of them and not let go. Guess what? These thoughts are not you and are not manufactured by you. Let that sink in. *These thoughts are not you and are not manufactured by you.* So what are they, where did they come from, and why do they appear?

There are a few reasons why we tend to think negatively. One has to do with the way our brains are wired. The brain's default setting is to think negative because it's the way we were designed as humans. It evolved that way for good reason: our ancestors had a better chance for survival by honing in on the negative. The brain's hardware is mainly operated by two very simple, yet ancient, systems: the amygdala, which activates emotions for both negative and positive events, and the frontal cortex, which helps us to interpret events. Cognitive distortions, also known as mentally deformed thoughts (we call them *hope-hacking thoughts*) play an enormous role in our lives, especially when it comes to our mental health. These hope-hacking thoughts are the kinds of thoughts that our minds lead us to believe are true, when they are interpretations that may or may not be factual.

In addition to worry, there are other kinds of hope-hacking thoughts that can easily induce anxiety. Some common ones are catastrophizing, perfectionism, negative and pessimistic thinking, and obsessions or compulsions that keep you stuck in an anxiety loop constantly repeating thoughts and behaviors. When life is full of chronic, unrelenting stressors, and when our minds are kind of worn down by all the mental mayhem that constantly happens to us, that's when our hope-hacking thoughts start to take a real toll on us.

Our thinking is shaped not only by what's happening in our brains, but by society, culture, media messages, and the influences of our environment, family, and friends. As Jim Rohn famously said, "You are the average of the five people you spend the most time with," which highlights how the people around us play a significant role in shaping our thoughts and behaviors. To break down hope-hacking thinking, be aware that these are things that shape the thoughts that pop in our heads. Awareness is the first step towards change.

HOW:
Learn a Tool for Thriving

How can we change our operating system to have automatic hope-filled thoughts instead of hope-hacking thoughts? (By the way, don't be too hard on yourself. We all have these, and we are all a work in progress.) We will use the Catch-and-Release Model to work one hope-hacking thought one step at a time and watch joy come in one thought at a time

Step 1: Catch

+ **Recognize.** We must first learn which thoughts are hope-filled and which are hope-hacking. Once you realize there is a hope-hacker trying to hack in your system; then...

+ **Stop.** Stop it dead in its tracks! Don't let it race around in your mind, over and over and over (rumination). This is chaotic and makes you feel completely out of control.

Step 2: Release

+ **Analyze.** Write it down at first-at least visualize it for this next part.

+ **Put it on trial.** Is this thought fact or fiction?

+ **Collect evidence.** What evidence is there that makes this a fact or fiction? For example, is there a bear chasing you, or is the thought a what if there was a bear chasing you. Do you see a real bear?

- **If it is fact,** then deal with it; run as fast as you can!

- **If it is fiction,** then release it. Let it go, and don't hold it any longer.

Step 3: Rinse

- **Flip the script.** Flip the hope-hacking thought to a hope-filled thought. It must be hope-filled, attainable (not just a fairy tale!), encouraging, motivating, and actionable.

Step 4: Repeat

Here is an example of Catch, Release, Rinse, Repeat:
Catch, Release, Rinse, and Repeat Sample

CATCH	
	I notice myself thinking, 'There's too much to do—I'll never get it all done.' This thought is making me feel overwhelmed and stuck.
RELEASE	
	I pause and take a deep breath. I challenge this thought. Is it fact or just stress talking? I remind myself that I don't have to do everything at once.
RINSE	
	I reframe the thought: 'I can take one step at a time and prioritize what truly matters.' I focus on progress, not perfection.
REPEAT	
I practice this shift daily, reinforcing the belief that small steps lead to big progress. Over time, I train my brain to focus on what I *can* do instead of what feels impossible.	

Examples of Flipping the Script

1. **All-or-Nothing Thinking (Polarized Thinking):** Seeing things in extremes, with no shades of gray.

   - » **Hope-Hacking Thought:** "I messed up this presentation. I'm a complete failure."
   - » **Hope-Filled Thought:** "The presentation didn't go perfectly, but I can learn from my mistakes and improve next time."

2. **Overgeneralization:** Taking one negative event and applying it to everything.

   - » **Hope-Hacking Thought:** "I got rejected for this job. I'll never get a good job."
   - » **Hope-Filled Thought:** "This job application wasn't successful, but there are many other opportunities out there."

3. **Mental Filter:** Focusing only on the negative aspects of a situation and ignoring the positive ones.

   - » **Hope-Hacking Thought:** "My boss only mentioned my mistakes in my performance review."
   - » **Hope-Filled Thought:** "My boss mentioned areas for improvement and also acknowledged some strengths."

4. **Discounting the Positive:** Minimizing your accomplishments or positive experiences.

   - » **Hope-Hacking Thought:** "They only complimented my work because they felt bad for me."
   - » **Hope-Filled Thought:** "I received a compliment because my work was very good."

5. **Jumping to Conclusions (Mind Reading):** Assuming you know what someone else is thinking, without any concrete evidence.

   » **Hope-Hacking Thought:** "They're not talking to me. They must be mad at me."

   » **Hope-Filled Thought:** "I don't know why they're not talking to me, and I can always ask them directly."

6. **Jumping to Conclusions (Fortune Telling):** Predicting that things will turn out badly, without any relevant evidence.

   » **Hope-Hacking Thought:** "I'm going to bomb this interview."

   » **Hope-Filled Thought:** "I'm prepared for the interview, and I'm going to do my best."

7. **Magnification (Catastrophizing):** Blowing a negative event out of proportion and imagining the worst possible outcome.

   » **Hope-Hacking Thought:** "If I make a mistake at work, I'll get fired."

   » **Hope-Filled Thought:** "Everyone makes mistakes at work. If I do make one, I can apologize and learn from it."

8. **Minimization:** Making light of an unpleasant event or your feelings.

   » **Hope-Hacking Thought:** "It's not a big deal that I got passed over for the promotion." (when you secretly wanted it)

   » **Hope-Filled Thought:** "It's okay to feel disappointed about not getting the promotion. I will focus on what I can do to improve my chances next time."

9. **Emotional Reasoning:** Believing that your emotions reflect reality.

   » **Hope-Hacking Thought:** "I feel like a loser, so I must be a loser."

   » **Hope-Filled Thought:** "My feelings are valid, but they don't define who I am."

10. **Should Statements:** Holding yourself or others to unrealistic expectations using *should*, *ought to*, or *must*.

> » **Hope-Hacking Thought:** "I should be able to handle this perfectly."

> » **Hope-Filled Thought:** "It's okay to ask for help if I need it. I've taken the word *perfect* out of my vocabulary. I'll learn from my mistakes if I need to. I'm a work in progress. That's perfect!

11. **Labeling and Mislabeling:** Assigning negative labels to yourself or others based on a single mistake.

> » **Hope-Hacking Thought:** "I made a mistake. I'm such a careless idiot."

> » **Hope-Filled Thought:** "I made a mistake, but that doesn't mean I'm a bad person. Everyone makes mistakes. I will learn from mine."

12. **Personification:** Taking responsibility for events that are outside of your control.

> » **Hope Hacking Thought:** "If I had been more outgoing, my friend wouldn't have moved away."

> » **Hope-Filled Thought:** "My friend moved away for reasons of their own, and that's not something I can control."

13. **Control Fallacies:** Believing that you have control over everything or that you have no control at all.

> » **Hope-Hacking Thought:** "If I worry enough about something bad happening, I can prevent it."

> » **Hope-Filled Thought:** "I can control my own actions and reactions, but I can't control everything that happens."

14. **Fallacy of Fairness:** Believing that everything should be fair and that you are getting what you deserve.

> » **Hope-Hacking Thought:** "It's not fair that they got the promotion and I didn't."

> » **Hope-Filled Thought:** "I may not have gotten the promotion this time, but there will be other opportunities."

15. **Blaming:** Assigning fault to yourself or others for everything that goes wrong.

> » **Hope-Hacking Thought:** "It's all my fault we lost the game."

> » **Hope-Filled Thought:** "Everyone makes mistakes. Let's learn from this game and focus on what we can do better next time."

16. **Disqualification of the Positive:** Rejecting positive experiences because of a perceived flaw.

> » **Hope-Hacking Thought:** "Someone complimented my work, but they probably just said that to be nice."

> » **Hope-Filled Thought:** "I received a compliment because my work was so good. I will accept it graciously."

17. **Labeling:** Assigning global negative labels to yourself or others based on a single event or behavior.

> » **Hope-Hacking Thought:** "I forgot to call my friend back. I'm a terrible friend."

> » **Hope-Filled Thought:** "Forgetting to call someone back doesn't make me a terrible friend. I can apologize and make it up to them."

Repeat

We build our hope-operational thinking (HOT) by building hope habits. At first you will need to make a conscious effort to repeat the hope-filled thoughts. Remember, this takes time and practice (63 days to be exact). In fact, building our endurance to notice the hope-hacking thoughts is, in and of itself, a big breakthrough.

We often don't even realize we are entertaining hope-hacking thoughts. It usually takes focused practice to flip the script because these thoughts might be entirely new to us. Also, we may need help to even know what hope-filled thoughts to use to replace the hope-hacking thoughts. But, it is worth it!

This is the area where you will spend the most time and reap the most valuable gains! Hope doesn't activate in isolation. Without endurance hope fades. Endurance is what makes hope sustainable. We learn endurance with the help of hope. When hope is lost, endurance becomes passivity (Rich 2021). With practice, the hope-filled thought will become the automatic thought in time and will no longer take that focused energy. Endurance is vital.

WHY:
Understand the Importance

Imagine your brain is a supercomputer, constantly learning and updating itself based on the thoughts you feed it. The more you focus on fear and doubt, the stronger those neural pathways become. Here's the good news: you can flip the script and rewire your brain for hope, success, and resilience!

Increasing your hope-filled self-talk is like upgrading your mental software: it strengthens the part of your brain that helps you tackle challenges, find solutions, and stay motivated. The coolest part? Your brain can change at any age! Those old hope-hacking messages are simply outdated programming. You have the power to rewrite them!

The key is to keep it real. Hope-filled thoughts aren't about ignoring challenges or pretending everything is perfect. Instead, they're about seeing yourself achieving your goals and taking action to make it happen. By shifting from "I can't" to "I'm doing what it takes," you're training your brain to be a problem-solving machine.

The reality is, 90 percent of your thoughts are repetitive, so whatever you repeat often enough becomes a habit. If your hope-hacking thoughts take over, they can shape how you see yourself and your potential. If you flip the script to hope-filled thoughts, you can create powerful, habitual hope habits that drive success.

Think of your brain like a computer operating system. Your experiences, environment, and past messages all make up your programming. If you let hope-hacking thoughts run the show, it's like clicking on a virus link that corrupts your system. On the other hand, if you choose hope-filled thoughts, you're installing a stronger, more resilient mindset that can lead you to success, happiness, and balance.

As Alain de Botton says, "The difference between hope and despair is a different way of telling stories from the same facts." That's the power of Hope-Operational Thinking (HOT, HOT, HOT!)—rewiring your brain to see possibilities, take action, and create a better future!

Here are some benefits of flipping the script to hope-filled thinking:

+ Strengthens problem-solving skills and resilience.

+ Rewires the brain for success, motivation, and positivity.

+ Encourages self-belief and unlocks potential.

+ Maintains a realistic, actionable mindset without false optimism.

+ Reinforces self-worth and confidence.

+ Helps recognize challenges while focusing on solutions.

+ Prevents negative thought loops from becoming habits.

+ Promotes emotional balance and mental well-being.

Which type of thinking would you prefer: hope-hacking or hope-filled? The choice is yours. And don't worry, we're on this journey with you! As Best Questers, we're here to help you build the mindset, habits, and strategies that will bring more joy, success, and resilience into your life. Let's do this—together!

SCIENCE BEHIND THE STRATEGY: Research for Practical Impact

It takes 63 days to develop a habit (Leaf 2021). During this process, the dendrites in your brain where memories and thoughts are stored begin to change. At day 63 of using the new thought, the new thought moves into your unconscious mind and becomes a habit. Just like a house that gets a makeover and is flipped, imagine giving your thinking a major renovation. Renovations take time, but they are worth it. We can upgrade our hope-hacked operational system for a new and improved hope-filled system that is transformed, empowered, and incredibly powerful.

Flipping the script—replacing negative self-talk with hope-filled thoughts—is supported by research in psychology, neuroscience, and cognitive behavioral therapy (CBT). Below are key scientific principles that explain why this strategy works:

Thought rewiring

+ The brain has the ability to reorganize itself by forming new neural connections based on repeated thoughts and behaviors (Doidge 2007).

+ Empowering self-talk strengthens neural pathways associated with resilience and problem-solving, while hope-hacking self-talk reinforces stress and anxiety (Davidson and McEwen 2012).

Hope-hacking thoughts

+ The way we think affects how we feel and act (Beck 1976).

+ Reframing hope-hacking thoughts into more empowering, hope-filled perspectives that can reduce anxiety and depressive symptoms (Burns 1980).

Thought-to-reality outcomes

+ The way we talk to ourselves can shape our results, either strengthening self-doubt or enhancing performance (Merton 1948).

+ When individuals shift to perceptions that serve them well, they are more likely to take proactive steps toward success (Rosenthal and Jacobson 1968).

The role of the brain in emotional responses

+ Repeated exposure to hope-hacking self-talk triggers stress responses, whereas hope-filled thoughts help regulate emotional reactivity in the brain (Fredrickson 2001).

The 63-day habit-formation process

+ Research suggests it takes approximately 63 days to form a lasting habit, including thought patterns (Leaf 2021).

+ Consistently practicing empowering self-talk can help replace deeply in-grained hope-hacking thoughts over time.

Hope theory, resilience, and emotional well-being

+ Snyder's Hope Theory states that hope consists of goal-directed thinking, agency (motivation), and pathways (solutions) (Snyder 2002).

+ Individuals who practice hope-filled thinking demonstrate higher resilience and improved emotional well-being (Cheavens et al. 2005).

Gratitude and positive psychology

+ Expressing gratitude and focusing on empowering self-talk can increase levels of dopamine and serotonin, neurotransmitters linked to happiness and emotional stability (Emmons and McCullough 2003).

+ Positive psychology emphasizes strengths-based approaches to improve well-being (Seligman 2011).

MEET THE TEACHER:
Real-Life Application

Mr. Navarro slammed his overflowing lab coat drawer shut, the clatter echoing through the cluttered science classroom. A rogue test tube skittered across the counter, coming to rest beside a growing pile of ungraded papers and half-eaten granola bars. Burnout, a familiar foe, clung to him like a wet shirt.

Middle school science—once a thrilling whirlwind of bubbling beakers, erupting volcanoes, and electrified curiosity—now felt like a battlefield, littered with the casualties of impossible expectations as far as the eye could see. Standardized tests loomed, demanding a relentless focus on rote memorization (the dang periodic table again!), choking the life out of scientific discovery. Meanwhile, his inbox overflowed with emails about committee meetings, parent conferences, and yet another online training—this time on lab safety and the mating habits of the common fruit fly.

I should be able to handle all of this. I feel like such a failure, Mr. Navarro thought, the pressure tightening in his chest.

His students, once a source of endless fascination, now felt like a burden. Their low test scores, a constant reminder of his perceived shortcomings, fueled his self-doubt. A forgotten permission slip morphed into proof of nonexistent parental support, a reflection of his inadequate communication skills. *If only I had explained the deadline more clearly,* he thought, guilt gnawing at him.

A whispered joke during a dissection suddenly felt like an attack on his teaching. *Don't they respect me? Don't they care about learning about these amazing creatures?* His frustration simmered, threatening to boil over.

The passion that once lit up his classroom now flickered, struggling against the weight of frustration, exhaustion, and doubt.

A TEACHER'S MEMOIR:
Learn from Others

I sank into my chair, exhaustion pressing down on me like a weight I couldn't shake. My shoulders ached, my mind was foggy, and the day had drained every ounce of energy I had left. I can't keep doing this. The thought hit like a dagger, one of many that had been creeping in lately. Teaching had become a relentless cycle of pushing through, running on empty, and wondering if I even made a difference anymore.

Then, a teacher at my school recommended High Five to Thrive, *saying it had completely changed the way she handled stress. She mentioned a tool called Catch, Release, Rinse, and Repeat, but as soon as I heard the steps, it sounded too difficult to even try. I could barely keep up with my workload—how was I supposed to monitor every negative thought and reframe it? It felt like just another thing to add to my already overwhelming to-do list. But I was desperate. Something had to change. If I didn't shift my thinking, burnout wasn't just a possibility; it was inevitable. I told myself I had nothing to lose and finally persuaded myself to give it a try.*

CATCH: *I noticed the thought creeping in: I should be able to handle all of this. That "should" statement was setting an impossible standard, dragging me deeper into self-doubt.*

STOP: *I paused, took a deep breath, and reminded myself that this thought wasn't helpful. It was just fueling my exhaustion.*

RELEASE: *I put the thought on trial. Was it fact, or just a harsh narrative I'd built up? I thought back to last week's astronomy lesson—my students debating black holes with genuine excitement. They were engaged. They were learning. That moment was proof that I was making an impact.*

RINSE: *I flipped the script. I can't do everything perfectly, but I can find better ways to manage my workload. I can create engaging lessons without burning out.*

REPEAT: *The cycle started again.*

When I caught myself thinking, If I had just explained the permission slip deadline more clearly... I paused. Was that entirely on me? Several students had asked about the trip earlier, proving they had heard me. I let go of the guilt and reframed the thought: I can send a reminder email and set up a better system next time.

Then came the toughest thought: Do these kids even respect me? Do they even care about science? I stopped myself. I was assuming what they thought without any proof. I remembered a student's specific question about an experiment—clear evidence of curiosity and engagement. I replaced my doubt with a more hopeful thought: Maybe they process information differently today, and I can try a new approach tomorrow.

This wasn't just positive thinking—it was science, and I read about it in High Five to Thrive. *The book explained that if we repeatedly replace negative thoughts with positive ones, our brains start to rewire. It takes a long time for new thought habits to become natural, but each time we catch ourselves and flip the script, the new thought habit gets more automatic.*

With each small success, I felt my mindset shifting. My brain was slowly rewiring itself for resilience. My internal system was upgrading from stress-driven survival mode to something stronger—hope and empowerment. I wasn't just trudging through the day anymore; I was reclaiming my energy, my confidence, and my purpose. For the first time in a long while, I felt like myself again. And that was enough.

Highlights of Mr. Navarro's Experience

Mr. Navarro's journey with the *Catch, Release, Rinse, and Repeat* tool marked a turning point in his teaching career. He hadn't realized how much his own thinking was fueling his exhaustion and stress—until he stepped back and examined his thought patterns. Once he recognized the impact of his mindset, he committed to trying a new approach, and the results were too powerful to ignore.

Rewiring Negative Thought Patterns

Mr. Navarro realized that negative thoughts fueled his stress and self-doubt.

- Research shows these patterns reinforce anxiety and burnout (Beck 1976; Burns 1980).

- By shifting to solution-focused thinking, he rewired his brain for resilience (Doidge 2007).

Pausing to Regain Control

He learned to stop and take a deep breath whenever negative thoughts spiraled, giving himself a moment to assess their accuracy instead of reacting emotionally.

- Mindful pauses help regulate emotions and reduce stress (Porges 2017).

- Releasing self-defeating thoughts prevented stress responses, promoting a calmer mindset (Fredrickson 2001).

Flipping the Script: From Doubt to Confidence

Mr. Navarro began questioning whether his self-doubt was based on facts or assumptions. Instead of thinking *I'm failing as a teacher*, he asked, *What evidence do I have to support or challenge this thought?*

- Reframing self-doubt boosted confidence and motivation (Merton 1948; Rosenthal and Jacobson 1968).

- Changing thought patterns strengthened resilience and success (Seligman 2011).

Regulating Emotional Responses

As he replaced self-criticism with constructive thoughts, he noticed a shift in how he handled challenges. Instead of frustration, he felt hope; instead of obstacles, he saw possibilities.

+ Releasing negativity and focusing on hope improves emotional control and clarity (Leaf 2021).

+ Hope-based thinking enhances problem-solving and resilience (Snyder 2002).

The 63-Day Habit Formation Process

Mr. Navarro committed to practicing this tool daily, even when it felt unnatural at first. Over time, positive thought replacement became more automatic.

+ New habits form in about 63 days as the brain adapts (Leaf 2021).

+ Repeating Catch, Release, Rinse, and Repeat strengthened his hopeful mindset.

Hope Theory, Resilience, and Teacher Well-being

This mindset shift transformed his teaching experience, helping him reconnect with his students, reignite his passion for education, and approach challenges with a sense of possibility rather than defeat.

+ Hope Theory links goal-setting, motivation, and problem-solving to resilience (Snyder 2002; Cheavens et al. 2005).

By consistently applying the Catch, Release, Rinse, and Repeat tool, Mr. Navarro ensured that his hopeful mindset became a lasting habit. Through small, intentional shifts in thinking, he rewired his approach thinking about teaching—and rediscovered the joy that had once inspired him to step into the classroom.

YOUR TURN:
Take Action for Traction

Scan to Unlock Bonus Content (Catch, Release, Rinse, Repeat)

Now, it's your turn. Remember, when hope-hacking thoughts creep in, use Catch, Release, Rinse, and Repeat to shift your mindset. Catch the thought and recognize its impact. Release it by questioning whether it's fact or just stress talking. Rinse by flipping the script with a hopeful, solution-focused perspective. Repeat this process daily to rewire your brain for resilience and confidence. Small shifts in thinking lead to lasting change, so start today and take control of your mindset!

Unlock this strategy and even more powerful strategies and exclusive resources at BestQuesters.net, where you thrive and grow with purpose and impact.

JOURNALING:
Reflect and Bloom

Scan to Unlock Bonus Content (Journaling-Reflect and Bloom)

REMEMBER, this page is for you to write down your feelings, struggles, successes, and anything you feel you need or want to process after reading this chapter. If you are not accustomed to journaling, you can:

1. **Start with a prompt.** If you're unsure where to begin, you can use these guided prompts:

   » Reflecting on your self-talk, have you noticed a shift toward more positive and encouraging internal dialogue? If so, what has helped?

   » What are the most effective techniques you've found for shifting negative self-talk to a more supportive mindset?

   » How do you plan to maintain or strengthen the habit of speaking to yourself with kindness and encouragement?

2. **Write freely and honestly.** Don't worry about grammar or structure. This is your space to express yourself openly.

3. **Make it your own.** Customize your journaling practice with doodles, pictures, bullet points, creative storytelling, or any format that helps you reflect and connect with your journey.

Take a deep breath, let your thoughts flow, and allow this space to support your growth and transformation.

COACHING QUESTIONS:
Sustain Growth

As a reminder:

Scan to Unlock Bonus Content- Sustain Growth)

+ **Write** down questions you still have about the content, yourself, your feelings, emotions, etc.

+ **Discuss** questions in small groups, in a book study, or with a friend.

+ **Email** Best Questers with your questions at any time (info@ bestquesters.net).

+ **Discuss** in coaching conversations in professional learning communities or working with a mentor to facilitate productive discussions and support.

Practice 4:
Mind-Body Harmony

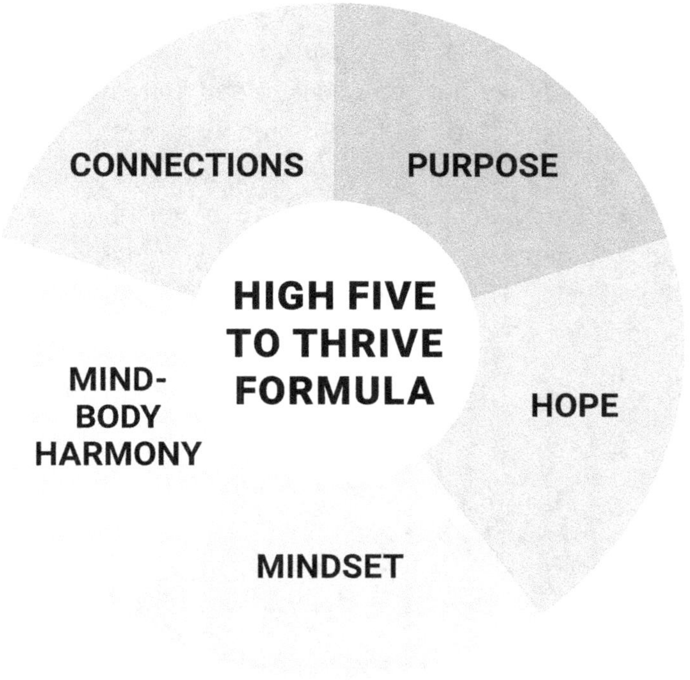

CONNECTIONS   PURPOSE

**HIGH FIVE
TO THRIVE
FORMULA**

MIND-
BODY
HARMONY

HOPE

MINDSET

WHAT:
Know the Problem

When you were considering the path of becoming an educator, you probably knew it wasn't going to be an easy job or one that guarantees financial stability. You might have been thinking about how you could shape the young minds of the future and support children in reaching their full potential. Choosing to become a teacher meant taking on an incredible, challenging, yet deeply meaningful, role. Life is hard sometimes, but it's also filled with joy—and being a teacher is no different.

It's also a journey filled with challenges you might not have anticipated. In the daily hustle, it's easy to get lost in the struggles and forget to tune into your body, mind, and spirit. If you take the time to truly listen, you may find the answers you need and deserve.

Like most teachers, you likely feel a mix of emotions as you prepare for the first day of school each year. Let's be honest—you might feel these emotions on any given school day! You may feel excited to meet your new students and their parents or worried about how administrative changes will affect you. You might feel hopeful about what the year or day will bring, or find yourself worrying about whether you'll be able to meet the unique needs of your students while balancing all the other demands of your job. This worry can sometimes hold you back, creating missed opportunities to truly connect and build partnerships with your students, parents, community, and colleagues.

The extraordinary demands placed on you as a teacher can be overwhelming. Every day, you're expected to greet your students with a smile and be on your game, but how in the world can you rise to the occasion every single day? Here's a strategy that is easy and effective.

HOW:
Learn a Tool for Thriving

What if you had a little kit to rise above the whirlwind of emotions and stress, that helped you relax, recharge, and regain balance in those tough moments? The Cool Calm Kit is your personalized toolkit to manage stress and keep your mind and body in sync. The more balanced we are, the more regulated our responses are to anything we encounter in our day. Are you ready to build your kit?

Let's break it down, step by step.

+ **Step 1:** Pick your sensory items.

+ **Step 2:** Add mindfulness tools.

+ **Step 3:** Incorporate positive affirmations.

+ **Step 4:** Include stress-relief activities.

+ **Step 5:** Personalize it with meaningful items.

+ **Step 6:** Put your Cool Calm Kit to use.

+ **Step 7:** Make it accessible and customize it.

Step 1: Pick your sensory items.

Your kit will focus on three senses—touch, smell, and sight—to create a holistic way to de-stress. Here's how to choose items for each sense:

+ **Touch: Ground yourself.**

  » **Soft, cuddly blanket:** Wrap yourself in a cozy blanket to provide comfort and warmth after a long day.

  » **Stress ball:** Squeeze it when you need to release tension and get your circulation going.

  » **Smooth stone or crystal:** Rub it between your fingers to calm your mind during stressful moments.

  » **Weighted blanket:** Allow the gentle pressure to help you feel grounded, supported, and relaxed.

  » **A piece of fabric that brings comfort:** Place the fabric between your fingertips and rub it. It does not have to be a big piece.

+ **Smell: Soothe your emotions.**

  » **Essential oil diffuser:** Use scents such as lavender, chamomile, or eucalyptus to promote relaxation. Use citrus essential oils to increase energy.

  » **Scented candle:** Choose a calming fragrance to instantly set a relaxing atmosphere.

  » **Incense sticks:** Light one up, take a few deep breaths, and let the aroma work its magic.

  » **Scented lotion or hand sanitizer:** Choose something as simple as a pleasant smell to help boost your mood.

+ **Sight: Reset your focus.**

> » **Nature photos or artwork:** Gather beautiful images of serene landscapes can reduce stress and bring calm.

> » **Inspirational quotes:** Keep a few quotes handy that remind you of your goals and values.

> » **Succulent or small plant:** Add a bit of greenery to improve your mood and even air quality in your space.

> » **Coloring book and colored pencils:** Try coloring as a fun way to unwind, get creative, and let your mind rest.

Step 2: Add mindfulness tools.

Mindfulness practices can make a huge difference in how you manage stress. Include a couple of these tools in your kit:

+ **Meditation app** (e.g., Calm or Headspace): Take advantage of easy access on your phone for guided meditation whenever you need it. These do not have to be long. They may be one or two minutes.

+ **Breathing exercises:** Use a quick script or guide for deep breathing exercises to instantly calm your nerves. Simply take five breaths in, hold, and then release.

+ **Guided imagery:** Keep a script or app that walks you through calming mental visuals

Step 3: Incorporate positive affirmations.

Positive affirmations remind you of your strength and purpose. Include a few of these:

+ **Inspirational quotes:** Pick ones that resonate with you and give you a mental boost.

+ **Personal mantras:** Write down a few mantras to remind yourself why you teach and the difference you're making.

+ **Affirmations:** Include notes from students that remind you of your worth and help you to feel valued.

Step 4: Include stress-relief activities.

Add a few activities that help you relax and recharge when things get hectic:

+ **Journal:** Write down your thoughts to clear your head or reflect on your day.

+ **Puzzles:** Use a fun and engaging way to shift focus and reset your brain.

+ **Short workout routines:** Create a list of quick exercises you can do during breaks to get your body moving.

+ **Body squeeze and release:** Tense up every muscle in your body, hold then release. Do this two or three times.

+ **Dance break:** Turn on your favorite song and dance!

Step 5: Personalize it with meaningful items.

Your kit should reflect you! Add a few personal touches:

+ **Photos of loved ones:** Choose a picture of your family, friends, or pets can bring comfort and joy.

+ **Favorite book or movie:** Find something that helps you unwind when you have downtime.

+ **Special objects:** Gather a keepsake or a gift that makes you smile— whatever brings you comfort.

Step 6: Put your calm kit to use.

Now that you've built your Cool Calm Kit, let's talk about how to use it during your busy teaching day. You can incorporate the kit into your routine like this:

+ **Start of the day:** Before school starts, take a few minutes to enjoy an item from your kit—maybe light a scented candle or diffuser, or spend a moment with a cozy blanket. This can set a positive tone for your day.

+ **During breaks:** In between classes or during a short break, use your kit to relax and recharge. Squeeze a stress ball, breathe in the scent of lavender, or simply gaze at a calming image.

+ **During planning periods:** When you're feeling stuck or need a mental boost, engage with a creative activity such as coloring or reflecting on an inspirational quote. Integrative practices go beyond mere stress reduction, addressing the deeper layers of personal and professional growth. Contemplative activities like reflective journaling not only provide immediate relief from tension but foster a more profound connection between body and mind, enhancing overall well-being.

+ **After school:** Unwind after the day with a moment for yourself. Wrap up in a blanket, light a candle, journal about your day to de-stress or play music.

Step 7: Make it accessible and customize it.

Keep your Cool Calm Kit somewhere convenient so you can easily access it when you need it. And remember, your kit should grow with you. Swap out items, add new tools, and experiment with what works best for you over time. Customize it to fit your individual needs and preferences. You may even create a small kit that will fit into your bag, so you can take it with you. This mini kit may contain a favorite smell, a picture, and a favorite touch item. This will enable access to your calming tools even on the go.

By following this step-by-step process, you'll have a personalized Cool Calm Kit ready to help you manage stress, boost focus, and enhance your overall well-being. Keep it with you, and whenever the day gets overwhelming, take a moment to dive into your kit—it'll make a world of difference. Happy teaching!

WHY: Understand the Importance

The Cool Calm Kit is a self-care strategy designed to help you manage stress, improve focus, regulate emotions, and enhance overall job satisfaction. When your mind and body are in sync, you're better equipped to handle challenges, boost your immune system, and even improve sleep quality.

Too often, we rush through the day without listening to what our mind and body need. Taking a short moment to pause, reset, and engage your senses can completely reshape your perspective and help you bring your best energy to your classroom.

The kit should include items that engage three key senses:

- **Touch** – Holding a textured item can ground you in the present moment, a core element of mindfulness that reduces anxiety and calms the mind.

- **Smell** – Certain scents, like lavender or peppermint, are scientifically shown to promote relaxation and mental clarity.

- **Sight** – Visual cues like calming colors or peaceful imagery can enhance focus, creativity, and mental reset.

Let's be real—teaching is demanding, and keeping your cool isn't always easy. But when you're calm and centered, you can handle student behaviors more effectively, create a positive classroom environment, and bring your best energy to your lessons. And guess what? Your students feel it, too! A relaxed teacher leads to more engaged students, deeper learning, and a smoother day overall.

Prioritizing your mind-body connection isn't just a nice idea, it's essential for long-term job satisfaction and fulfillment. The Cool Calm Kit is more than a stress-management tool—it's about emotional regulation, resilience, and mental stamina. When you take care of yourself, you're investing in your ability to keep showing up as the amazing educator you are.

And the best part? This isn't just about stress relief; it's about rewiring your brain for success. Mind-body tools don't just lower stress hormones; they also enhance cognitive function. Think:

- Clearer thinking

- Sharper memory

- More focus and energy

Basically, you're activating superhero brain mode!

Here are some benefits of using the Cool Calm Kit:

- Reduces stress and improves emotional regulation.

- Strengthens resilience, helping you handle challenges with ease.

- Boosts focus, creativity, and cognitive function.

- Enhances mental and physical well-being, including better sleep.

- Creates a more positive classroom environment, benefiting both teachers and students.

+ Promotes mindfulness and self-care, leading to higher job satisfaction.

+ Helps rewire the brain for long-term emotional balance and success.

Dive into the magic of mind-body mojo! Your students will thank you. You will thank you.

SCIENCE BEHIND THE STRATEGY: Research for Practical Impact

The Cool and Calm Kit is based on research in neuroscience, psychology, and stress management. Below are key scientific principles that explain why this strategy is effective in helping teachers and students regulate emotions and maintain balance.

Sensory regulation and the nervous system

+ Engaging the senses (touch, sight, smell) helps regulate the autonomic nervous system, reducing stress and promoting relaxation (Porges 2011).

+ The Polyvagal Theory explains how sensory input can shift the body from a state of stress (sympathetic nervous system activation) to a state of calm (parasympathetic activation) (Dana 2018).

Mindfulness and stress reduction

+ Mindfulness practices, such as deep breathing and grounding techniques, have been shown to lower cortisol levels and improve emotional regulation (Kabat-Zinn 1990).

+ Studies indicate that mindfulness helps individuals become more aware of their emotions and enhances their ability to manage stress effectively (Goyal et al. 2014).

Cognitive Behavioral Therapy (CBT) and thought regulation

+ CBT techniques, such as self-talk and cognitive reframing, help individuals rewire negative thought patterns and improve resilience (Beck 1976).

+ Tools in the Cool and Calm Kit (such as affirmations and visualization exercises) are grounded in CBT principles that promote positive thinking and stress reduction (Burns 1980).

Aromatherapy and emotional regulation

+ Certain essential oils, such as lavender and peppermint, have been scientifically shown to reduce anxiety and improve mood by influencing the limbic system (Koulivand et al. 2013).

+ The use of scent-based interventions in classrooms has been linked to increased focus and decreased stress in students (Howard and Hughes 2016).

Tactile stimulation and stress reduction

+ Engaging in fidgeting behaviors (such as using stress balls or textured objects) can improve concentration and reduce stress levels by providing a physical outlet for nervous energy (Baker 2018).

+ Research on deep pressure stimulation (such as weighted blankets or soft textures) has shown benefits for individuals with anxiety and sensory processing challenges (Grandin 1992).

Breathing techniques and physiological calm

+ Slow, deep breathing activates the vagus nerve, which promotes relaxation and emotional stability (Jerath et al. 2006).

+ The 4-7-8 breathing technique and other structured breathing exercises help regulate heart rate and reduce stress-induced physiological responses (Brown and Gerbarg 2012).

Grounding techniques and anxiety management

+ 5-4-3-2-1 grounding exercises (focusing on five senses) have been shown to help individuals shift from anxiety to the present moment (Niles et al. 2018).

+ Grounding practices are effective in reducing symptoms of stress-related disorders, including PTSD and generalized anxiety disorder (Zerach et al. 2020).

Gratitude and positive psychology

+ Expressing gratitude through journaling or reflection improves overall emotional well-being by shifting focus from stress to positive experiences (Emmons and McCullough 2003).

+ Gratitude-based interventions have been linked to increased resilience and reduced burnout in educators (Chan 2011).

MEET THE TEACHER:
Real-Life Application

Mrs. Tanaka had always been known for her calm presence in the classroom, but lately, she was struggling. Her third graders were a lively bunch—full of energy, curiosity, and, unfortunately, endless distractions. No matter what tools she tried, the days felt more chaotic than controlled. She found herself exhausted, snapping at small things, and leaving work feeling drained. Something had to change. That's when she stumbled upon the idea of the Cool Calm Kit.

At first, it seemed too simple to make a difference. As she built her own kit—selecting small, meaningful items that helped her reset—she noticed a shift. She felt more grounded, more in control, and more like the teacher she wanted to be. When a colleague noticed the change and asked her to share at a faculty meeting, she hesitated. Could something this small really help others the way it had helped her? She decided to find out.

A TEACHER'S MEMOIR:
Learn from Others

A few months ago, I hit a breaking point. There always seemed to be more piled on my plate, and the constant noise, interruptions, and stress of the classroom were wearing me down. One afternoon, after a particularly chaotic day, I found myself venting to a friend who worked as a school counselor. "I just don't know how to keep up," I admitted. That's when she told me about the Cool Calm Kit—a simple tool inspired by Dialectical Behavioral Therapy designed to help manage stress through mindfulness and balanced thinking. Desperate for relief, I decided to give it a try.

I gathered a few meaningful items: a soft piece of cloth that reminded me of a childhood blanket, a small bottle of lavender essential oil to help me slow down, and a photo of my favorite beach in Okinawa. I placed these in a pretty bag and strategically set out similar items around my classroom. For instance, I kept a stress ball on a high shelf near the door to use when leading my class, knowing that even a small tactile stimulus can ease anxiety. My friend also joined as a supportive agent, sharing suggestions and encouragement along the way.

The Cool Calm Kit is built on solid scientific principles. Engaging my senses—whether it was the comforting touch of the cloth, the soothing aroma of lavender, or the serene sight of a beach—helped regulate my nervous system, shifting me from a state of stress to a state of calm. Mindfulness techniques like deep breathing and grounding exercises lowered my stress levels and made me more aware of my emotions. Using tools based on cognitive behavioral therapy, such as affirmations and visualization, helped me rewire my negative thought patterns into more balanced, positive ones. Even holding a stress ball provided the tactile stimulation needed to refocus my energy and improve concentration.

I also practiced structured breathing techniques that regulated my heart rate and activated my relaxation response, while grounding exercises anchored me in the present moment. Over time, expressing gratitude through these practices shifted my focus from stress to positive experiences, boosting my overall emotional well-being and resilience.

Whenever I felt overwhelmed, I'd glance at a peaceful image or quote on my wall, or reach for an item in my kit—a soothing scent or a soft, comforting cloth. I came to favor the lavender oil and the Okinawa photo, which reminded me to take deep breaths and slow down to a healthier pace. Gradually, I began to emerge from reactive mode. I felt more in control, my outlook improved, and my students even seemed to pick up on my calmer energy. The atmosphere in our classroom became noticeably more peaceful and upbeat.

Then came the faculty meeting. The principal had asked me to share my experience. I was hesitant at first, but as I stood in front of my colleagues, holding up my Cool Calm Kit, I saw curiosity in their eyes. "I know it seems small," I told them, "but this little bag has changed my entire approach to stress and restored my peace. Your kit doesn't have to look like mine, but having something tangible to help you reset can make all the difference." I could see the wheels turning in their minds—maybe, just maybe, this was something that could help them, too.

By embracing the science behind sensory regulation, mindfulness, CBT, aromatherapy, tactile stimulation, breathing, grounding, and gratitude, I upgraded my stress management system. The Cool Calm Kit has become my lifeline—a constant reminder that a few mindful, intentional actions can transform stress into calm, and chaos into balance.

Highlights of Mrs. Tanaka's Experience

Mrs. Tanaka shared a personal and transformative experience with the Cool Calm Kit, demonstrating its effectiveness as a practical tool for managing stress and improving classroom dynamics. Below are the key highlights of what she learned, along with the scientific principles that support them:

Sensory regulation and nervous system

+ During a stressful moment, Mrs. Tanaka realized she needed to take action to prevent losing her composure.

+ This response aligns with research on sensory regulation, which shows that engaging the senses helps shift the autonomic nervous system from a state of stress to calm (Porges 2011; Dana 2018).

Mindfulness and stress reduction

+ Despite initial doubts, she chose to give the Cool and Calm Kit a chance.

+ This decision reflects the benefits of mindfulness practices, which lower cortisol levels and improve emotional regulation (Kabat-Zinn 1990; Goyal et al. 2014).

Cognitive Behavioral Therapy (CBT) and thought regulation

+ As her stress faded, her thinking became clearer, and she felt much more in control.

+ This shift mirrors findings from cognitive behavioral therapy, where reframing negative thoughts leads to improved emotional regulation (Beck 1976; Burns 1980).

Aromatherapy and emotional regulation

+ Using lavender essential oil, she felt a wave of relaxation as the calming scent slowed her racing thoughts and relieved anxiety.

+ This is consistent with studies showing that aromatherapy can reduce anxiety and improve mood by influencing the limbic system (Koulivand et al. 2013; Howard and Hughes 2016).

Tactile stimulation and stress reduction

+ Holding a small textured stone helped her refocus and calm her nerves.

+ Engaging with tactile sensory items, such as fidget tools or soft textures, can reduce stress and improve concentration by providing a physical outlet for nervous energy (Baker 2018; Grandin 1992).

Breathing techniques and physiological calm

+ Taking slow, deep breaths helped her physically relax, slowing her heart rate and clearing her mind.

+ Deep breathing techniques, such as the 4-7-8 method, activate the vagus nerve, promoting relaxation and emotional stability (Jerath et al. 2006; Brown and Gerbarg 2012).

Grounding techniques and anxiety management

+ Looking at a picture of the beach allowed her to mentally escape to a peaceful place, further calming her mind and emotions.

+ Visualization and grounding techniques, such as the 5-4-3-2-1 exercise, help shift attention from anxiety to the present moment, reducing stress-related symptoms (Niles et al. 2018; Zerach et al. 2020).

Gratitude and positive psychology

+ By committing to her self-care routine, she experienced tangible benefits that improved her overall well-being.

+ This highlights the impact of gratitude and positive psychology in reducing burnout and enhancing resilience (Emmons and McCullough 2003; Chan 2011).

Enlisting a Hope Agent

+ With the support and accountability of a trusted friend, Mrs. Tanaka experienced a boost in hope levels—a key factor in reinforcing positive behavior and reducing stress through social support (Chan 2011).

Encouraging others to create their own kit

+ Inspired by her transformation, Mrs. Tanaka shared the power of the Cool and Calm Kit with her colleagues.

+ This ripple effect demonstrates how effective stress management and mindfulness strategies can improve both mental health and social dynamics in educational settings (Kabat-Zinn 1990; Goyal et al. 2014).

YOUR TURN:
Take Action for Traction

Build your personalized Cool Calm Kit to manage stress, find balance, and recharge throughout the day. Fill in each section with items and activities that work best for you, targeting your senses, connection, and mindfulness needs.

Touch: Ground Yourself

Choose items that provide a calming sensation or help you feel connected to the present moment.

- Soft, cuddly blanket
- Stress ball
- Smooth stone or crystal
- A piece of fabric that brings comfort

Smell: Soothe Your Emotions

Include scents that relax or uplift you, helping to regulate your emotions throughout the day.

- Essential oil or scent
- Scented candle or incense
- Scented lotion or hand sanitizer
- Scented marker or scratch-n sniff sticker

Sight: Reset Your Focus

- Pick visual items that bring you calm and help you refocus when needed.
- Calming visual
- Inspirational quotes or mantras

Add Mindfulness Tools

Add items that support mindfulness and help you stay present, calm, and focused.

+ Meditation app

+ Breathing exercises

+ Guided imagery

Positive Affirmations: Boost your Mindset

Incorporate quotes, mantras, or affirmations that inspire and motivate you.

+ Inspirational quotes

+ Personal mantras

+ Affirmations

Stress-Relief Activities

Add activities that help you de-stress, be creative, and unwind.

+ Coloring book

+ Journal

+ Puzzles

+ Short workout routines

+ Body squeeze and release

+ Dance break

Meaningful Items

Bring in items that have personal significance and help you feel connected and comforted.

+ Photos of loved ones

+ Favorite book or movie

+ Special objects

How to Use Your Cool Calm Kit

Fill in your plan for using your kit throughout your teaching day

Start of the day: _____

During breaks: _____

During planning periods: _____

After school: _____

Scan to Unlock Bonus Content (Cool Calm Kit)

Customize and evolve your Cool Calm Kit as needed to fit your preferences. Keep it handy and use it throughout the day to stay centered, relaxed, and ready to tackle whatever comes your way!

Unlock this strategy and even more powerful strategies and exclusive resources at BestQuesters.net, where you thrive and grow with purpose and impact.

JOURNALING:
Reflect and Bloom

Scan to Unlock Bonus Content (Journaling- Reflect and Bloom)

REMEMBER, this page is for you to write down your feelings, struggles, successes, anything you feel you need or want to process after reading this chapter. If you are not accustomed to journaling, you can:

1. **Start with a prompt**. If you're unsure where to begin, you can use these guided prompts:

» What changes have you made in your self-care practices since beginning this journey?

» Do you feel more in control of your emotional and physical wellness now? If so, what has contributed to that change? If not, what additional tools might you explore?

» How do you plan to maintain your commitment to well-being, even during stressful times?

2. **Write freely and honestly.** Don't worry about grammar or structure. This is your space to express yourself openly.

3. **Make it your own.** Customize your journaling practice with doodles, pictures, bullet points, creative storytelling, or any format that helps you reflect and connect with your journey.

Take a deep breath, let your thoughts flow, and allow this space to support your growth and transformation.

COACHING QUESTIONS: Sustain Growth

As a reminder:

Scan to Unlock Bonus Content (Coaching Questions- Sustain Growth)

+ **Write** down questions you still have about the content, yourself, your feelings, emotions, etc.

+ **Discuss** questions in small groups, in a book study, or with a friend.

+ **Email** Best Questers with your questions at any time (info@bestquesters.net).

+ **Discuss** in coaching conversations in professional learning communities or working with a mentor to facilitate productive discussions and support.

Practice 5: Connections

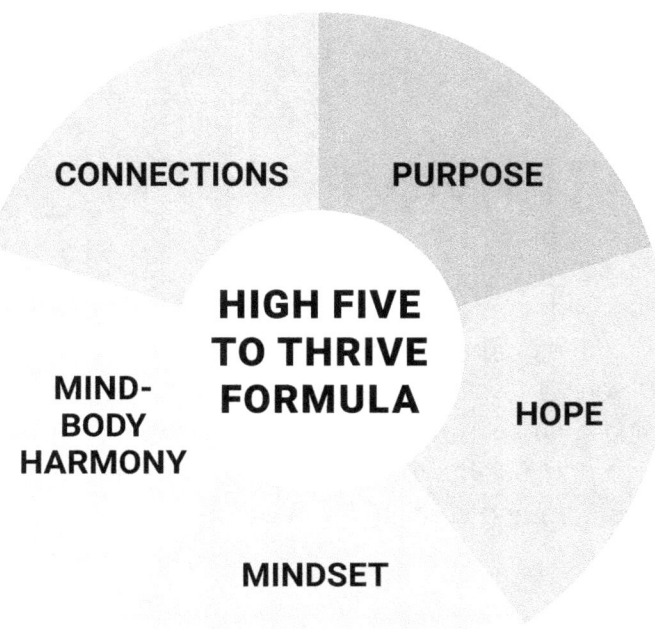

WHAT:
Know the Problem

The inner work we've been doing so far is super important because, well, you matter. The benefits, however, extend beyond you, and that's also important since other people matter, too. In this chapter we delve into cultivating positive relationships to further improve our own mental health while contributing to the well-being of others. Nurturing a supportive and uplifting social network is essential for a more positive and impactful school (and life) experience.

While we benefit immensely from good relationships, skillful connectors know that connecting is all about others. It is rooted in a guiding principle of John Maxwell and his Leadership Team which is that "we are people of value who value people and add value to them (Cole 2022)."

Connecting goes beyond just knowing someone. It means the ability to identify with others and relate to them in a way that builds trust and creates a bond (Maxwell 2010). That bond increases our influence, which is at the heart of living out our calling to make a difference. Highly successful people know how to leverage the power of connection, instinctively sensing that there is a direct correlation between achievement and the ability to care for and connect with others.

HOW:
Learn a Tool for Thriving

The Teacher Connection Plan is your roadmap for turning your classroom into a vibrant community. First up, you will lay the groundwork to create a welcoming, inclusive space for every student. Next, you will dive into creative, hands-on strategies to understand your students better and spark real, meaningful connections. Finally, you will reflect on your progress, gathering insights that help you grow as an educator. Ready to reimagine your classroom and connect like never before? Enjoy the journey!

Section 1: Explicitly Teach Expectations

If you are not a natural connector, you may be wondering what strategies you can use to connect with students and move them forward more effectively. A natural starting point is building a sense of security in the classroom by explicitly and systematically teaching and practicing class norms/expectations, evidence-based operating systems and behaviors, including micro-behaviors and most importantly showering your classroom with kindness and love.

These are rooted in our core value that proclaims we are all people of value who value people and add value to them. We do this with student buy-in, and we assess and reteach continually. Having highly effective and clearly defined operating procedures in place allows you to meet today's challenges with calm confidence and enthusiasm and create a caring, collaborative classroom where you and your students can bloom. When your students know what to expect each day their anxiety, emotional dysregulation and mental chatter subsides and behavior conducive to learning increases.

Reflection	Action Step	Action Plan
Reflect on your current classroom norms and how they foster a sense of security.	Develop and clearly communicate evidence-based expectations and behaviors, including micro-behaviors.	Systematically teach, model, and assess these norms daily, reteaching as needed to ensure all students feel valued and secure.

Section 2: Win Big with Rich Shared Experiences

Another way to foster connection and a sense of belonging is through rich shared experiences. You may already have some that serve this purpose but, if not, it's easy to tweak nearly any instructional activity to achieve both connecting *and* academic goals simultaneously. Find ways to acknowledge and celebrate students' small and big wins like we talked about in our Hope Action Plan. Pay particular attention to celebrating the things that reflect the values that facilitate the culture of belonging you are promoting, such as the following:

+ Accepting and encouraging one another

+ Demonstrating thoughtfulness, respect, and understanding

+ Diffusing a conflict or finding a win-win solution

+ Successfully collaborating with peers

+ Adhering to the group norms established by the class

Classroom rituals that focus on developing interpersonal and intrapersonal skills provide a valuable platform for sharing stories and experiences. They offer opportunities to model and teach students essential skills, such as valuing and honoring themselves and others. These rituals are venues to model and teach students how to disagree respectfully, listen to understand rather than to respond, and communicate to connect instead of to impress or correct. One-time activities, not just rituals or regularly occurring experiences, can bind us together and strengthen relationships as well!

These ideas can be accomplished within the context of your regular content instruction with little or no extra effort. (We're all about lightening your load!) You'll inspire students to embrace higher ideals and expectations by organically and authentically weaving them into conversations, activities, notes, and rituals. You undoubtedly have some phenomenal classroom rituals, routines and experiences in place. How can you leverage these to foster connections and a sense of togetherness?

Reflection	Action Step	Action Plan
Consider your existing shared experiences and classroom rituals. What's working?	Identify opportunities to tweak instructional activities so they also build connections. Celebrate both small and big wins that align with your classroom values.	Implement regular activities and rituals that acknowledge collaborative successes, encouraging a culture of respect, empathy, and teamwork.

Section 3: Communicate to Connect

Let's dive into another strategy that can move the needle for you: communicating to connect instead of to correct. Often, without even realizing it, we find ourselves communicating to correct instead of to connect. As a teacher, this can be like walking a tightrope since part of our job is to provide corrections. Some situations call for tough love. We can navigate these instances by clinging to our commitment to preserve the relationship, maintaining our inner peace and self-control, and communicating from a place of love and serenity. When a positive connection is well established and the person feels valued and cared for, the groundwork has been laid.

For example, if a student blurts out during a lesson, instead of saying, *"Stop interrupting,"* you might gently say, *"I love how excited you are to share. Let's make sure everyone gets a turn. I'll call on you in just a minute."* This small shift helps the student feel seen and valued, while still guiding them toward better behavior—**connection first, correction second.**

Here is a story of from one our authors, Debbie Simoes:

"In one particularly difficult season of my life, my sister said something that didn't feel good at that moment, but it was life-changing for me. She asked me if I knew what the common denominator was in all my problems. 'It's *you*,' she said. Ouch! She was right though, and her insight became an advantage for me. I tucked it away in my pocket and I still bring it out often so I can avoid being the common denominator ever again. I was able to accept her tough love because we had a caring relationship established, and she did not push me in the direction she thought I should go, but rather, she simply stated her observation without judgment and gave me the opportunity to reflect on it. She listened to understand, and she demonstrated empathy, so her tone and her actions reflected that she held me in high esteem and loved me enough to shine a light on my blind spot."

This example shows us how prioritizing connection over correction when correction is necessary can bring about a positive outcome.

Reflection	Action Step	Action Plan
Reflect on times when your communication felt more corrective than supportive.	Shift your focus from correcting to connecting by using empathetic language and active listening techniques.	Practice delivering feedback from a place of care and understanding, ensuring that even necessary corrections can maintain the integrity of the relationship.

Section 4: The Power of Praise

The Institute of Education Sciences identified teacher praise as one of the top five most effective practices for reducing behavior problems and maintaining instructional time (Waldinger and Schultz 2023). Effort-based and behavior-based praise help guide and reinforce specific actions, while noncontingent praise builds overall self-worth and belonging, and creates a positive classroom dynamic. It's like a secret weapon! Incorporating all types of praise can create a more balanced, encouraging environment and bring out the best in students. Of course, modeling non-contingent praise can have a powerful ripple effect.

Here's a breakdown of effort-based, behavior-based, and noncontingent praise with examples:

Effort-based praise. Praise that focuses on the effort a student puts into their work, rather than the outcome. Example: "Wow! I'm really impressed with how hard you worked on this project. Your dedication really shows!" This kind of praise encourages students to keep trying and reinforces the value of hard work.

Behavior-based praise. Praise that is linked directly to specific positive behaviors or actions. Example: "You did a great job raising your hand before speaking today. It helped keep our class discussions organized." This type of praise reinforces the behavior you want to see more of and helps students understand what actions are valued.

Noncontingent praise. Praise that is given freely and not tied to any specific behavior or achievement. It focuses on the student's qualities or general presence and is the most powerful of all praise because it is identity-based. Example: "I'm really glad you're here today. You bring such positive energy to our class!" This kind of praise helps build a student's self-esteem and makes them feel valued regardless of their actions or achievements.

The power of noncontingent praise includes building positive relationships, fostering self-esteem and a strong identity, and encouraging engagement and motivation. As a bonus, we're giving you our exclusive Praise Pack, a downloadable set of noncontingent praise cards that you can print out and use in a myriad of ways.

Scan to Unlock Bonus Content (Praise Pack)

Reflection	Action Step	Action Plan
Evaluate how your current praise practices impact student motivation and behavior.	Incorporate a balanced mix of effort-based, behavior-based, and non-contingent praise into your daily interactions.	Use tools like the exclusive Praise Pack to regularly recognize student achievements, reinforcing positive actions and boosting self-esteem.

Section 5: Focus on Common Ground

John Maxwell's Law of Attention says that whatever we focus on increases (Maxwell 2007). Conversely, whatever we don't focus on decreases. While it's important to appreciate and celebrate our uniqueness, to promote connection, we must look for and build on what we have in common. This brings everyone into the fold as valued and contributing members of the community—the ideal environment for high performance, regardless of whatever differences exist.

In fact, common ground is the place where people can share ideas, begin conversations about differences, find solutions, and start creating something together. The more people realize what they have in common, the better they can journey together. So, even if you only have 1 percent in common, give that 1 percent 100 percent!" In other words, give it your all.

Finding common ground is a practice of connecting. It requires us to think from others' perspectives and explore what matters to them. In a classroom setting, for example, the onus is on us to take the initiative to ask what our students see, feel, and want before expecting them to see, feel, and want what we see, feel, and want. Make a habit of being curious about them. Ask questions from the heart for the purpose of truly understanding what matters to them, what they dream about, what they cry about, what makes them sing, what their story is, how they interpret life, etc. People act on their own needs and for their own reasons. You connect with students when you are willing to lighten your grip on your own agenda and try to understand who they are and what matters to them. Connecting means making their agenda your agenda, meeting them where they are, not just academically but on a social/emotional level. The emotional context in which your message is heard is essential.

Reflection	Action Step	Action Plan
Reflect on what your students share in common, including interests, values, or challenges.	Identify shared interests and values that can serve as a foundation for classroom activities and discussions.	Design lessons and activities that highlight these commonalities, fostering collaboration and a sense of belonging among all students.

Section 6: Connecting Outside the Four Walls of Your Classroom

As you strengthen connections with your students, keep in mind that the same principles and practices can expand your influence beyond the classroom. By applying the same tools to building rapport with colleagues, school administrators, and parents, you create a network of support and collaboration that benefits everyone involved. You may be surprised at the doors this can open. Some teachers have received donations for their classroom, secured visits from guest speakers for their school, and created opportunities for students to serve and engage with the community beyond the school.

Incorporating connecting practices into your verbal and written communication with parents will build strong partnerships. AI can be a great tool to input your intended message and request a more polished version using language that communicates warmth, charisma, professionalism and a desire to collaborate. You can even ask AI to make a parent letter or newsletter culturally relevant to students' home culture. It is important for parents, teachers, administrators and students to understand that we are all on the same team working toward the success of the student. That begins with connecting.

Take the initiative to frame conversations with parents from the perspective of partnering together on behalf of the student rather than assume everyone is aware of this fundamental principle. Approaching challenges from a standpoint of working together for the student's success and seeking solutions together can strengthen home-school relationships. Creating opportunities for parent participation helps build a sense of community and strengthens families.

Similarly, you can level up your Professional Learning Community (PLC) with these same simple, yet powerful, connection tools. Start meetings with a quick, fun icebreaker or create a meaningful ritual, such as sharing "wins of the week" to set a positive tone. Make time for sharing personal teaching experiences. These moments build trust, encourage collaboration, and allow for peer coaching where you can learn from one another's successes and challenges. Don't overlook the power of recognition! Celebrating even the smallest achievements can boost morale, create a sense of progress, and raise hope levels. Try rotating a "shout-out" spotlight, where each team member highlights one colleague's contribution. Consider setting up a "takeaway board" where everyone writes down one practical idea they've gained after each meeting. What other small steps can you take to make your PLC a space where everyone feels valued and supported?

Consider reaching out to local businesses or community groups, inviting them to partner with your classroom. In fact, some parents who are business owners often like to partner with the school community. This could result in win-win outcomes, such as a business adopting your classroom, offering resources, time, or even funding for a special project or activity.

Serving the community can be very rewarding and help you and your students make a positive impact. The connections you foster today can open doors to opportunities that enrich not only your students' lives, but touch others' lives and your own as well.

Reflection	Action Step	Action Plan
Consider your current engagement with parents, colleagues, and community partners.	Develop strategies to extend connection practices beyond the classroom, creating a network of support.	Implement communication tools and community partnerships—such as icebreakers in PLCs and culturally relevant parent communications—to build strong, collaborative relationships.

Tying It All Together

You are probably connecting the dots already: the emotional well-being and hope agency addressed in previous chapters impact the depth and health of our relationships. In turn, healthy relationships are a major contributing factor to not just our success, but also our significance and ultimately, our happiness. Significance is a by-product of adding value to others and is a calling that stirs in the heart of every educator. Connecting, then, positions us to experience greater success, significance, happiness and health.

Keep in mind that people hear your words, but they *feel* your attitude. What you say accounts for only 7 percent of what people believe! The way we say it accounts for 38 percent, and what they see accounts for 55 percent. (Mehrabian 1971). In a nutshell, we must *be* the message we want to deliver. Nothing can happen through you until it happens *in* you, so begin each day by visualizing the teacher you want to be—the highest version of yourself. (Remember how we connected to our "why?") Then, commit fully to this identity and align your thoughts, actions and attitude as best you can. Just as you encourage your students to learn and grow step by step, remember that you are also on a journey of becoming an even better version of yourself, step by step.

The suggestions in this chapter boil down to embracing the notion that *"we are people of value who value people and add value to them,"* as John Maxwell lovingly reminds his team of leadership coaches often. Value and invest in yourself and others. Be intentional about making people feel special. Remember names, spend time with them, take an interest in them, have meaningful conversations about things that matter to them, share in their mistakes, failures, and successes, express gratitude, and one of my personal favorite tools, introduce others with infectious enthusiasm. As President Theodore Roosevelt famously said, "Nobody cares how much you know until they know how much you care." And as Maya Angelo poetically stated, "People will forget what you said, people will forget what you did, but people will never forget how you made them feel."

While the culture of our classrooms and schools is influenced by all the members of the community, never underestimate your power as a teacher—a classroom leader—to cultivate a culture of belonging and inspiration, a safe space where you and your students *love* stepping into your greatness together each day. James Clear, author of *Atomic Habits*, points out that, "People gravitate toward the standard you set, not the standard you request" (Clear 2018). By intentionally and consistently applying these practices, you can evolve as a person and as a teacher. Your impact will grow. You will show up differently, raising the minimum standard in your sphere of influence and creating a school experience that aligns with your calling and brings deep satisfaction, success, and significance.

WHY:
Understand the Importance

There's a happy upward spiral that happens. Self-care improves our emotional well-being, which paves the way for higher quality engagement and connection with others, which strengthens a sense of belonging and purpose.

This empowers us to serve more effectively and increases our impact, enjoyment and fulfillment, which then enhances our well-being even more. Here are a few more benefits of connecting, some of which may come as a surprise:

+ Expands possibilities

+ Improves sense of belonging

+ Strengthens community

+ Fosters feelings of safety and security

+ Promotes synergy

+ Builds motivation and buy-in

+ Increases effectiveness

+ Improves influence

+ Reduces discipline problems

+ Decreases conflict

+ Encourages risk-taking and learning by lowering the affective filter

+ Accelerates advancement and achievement

+ Facilitates longevity, good health, and well-being

A famous study by Harvard University followed 724 participants from all walks of life for 75 years. The researchers discovered that the participants who reported the highest levels of happiness and good health had just one thing in common: deep and satisfying relationships with others (Waldinger 2023). There are more benefits worth mentioning though!

Leaders who have learned the skill of connecting are able to establish buy-in and attract followers. That is because connecting increases influence, as we've mentioned, and influence is leadership. Legendary leadership expert John Maxwell calls this the Law of Influence, and it lies at the heart of teaching since nearly every teacher identifies with wanting to make a difference (Maxwell 2007). Is this true for you? Read on!

Connecting is not typically thought of as a skill that can be honed, but the good news is that, regardless of whether you're an introvert or an extrovert, or what your current ability level is, you can improve. Connecting is a skill worthy of developing since it is the key to making a difference in students' lives. It is also the key to making your job easier because it enables you to shift from managing students to leading them—the difference between pushing a rope and pulling a rope. Understanding the common-sense principles and best practices of connecting is a great starting point.

Building strong connections with your students can make a world of difference. When you get to know your students and create a genuine bond, you're setting up an environment where they feel safe, valued, and understood. This can make them more comfortable taking risks and participating in class activities.

When students know you genuinely care about them, they're more motivated and excited about learning. Behavior issues are minimized because kids are more likely to listen and respect someone they trust and look up to. Forging these strong relationships not only boosts academic performance and self-esteem but also makes a more positive school experience for everyone.

These ideas can be accomplished within the context of your regular content instruction with little or no extra work. You can inspire students to embrace higher ideals and expectations by organically and authentically weaving them into conversations, activities, notes, and rituals. There's no need to reinvent the wheel here or add more to your plate. How can you leverage things you are already doing to go beyond instructional goals to include the worthy goal of fostering connections and a sense of togetherness?

SCIENCE BEHIND THE STRATEGY: Research for Practical Impact

Building and maintaining meaningful connections is critical for personal well-being, professional success, and overall life satisfaction. Research in psychology, neuroscience, and education provides strong support for the importance of social connections.

The role of social connections in mental and physical health

+ Strong social relationships improve mental health, increase life satisfaction, and reduce the risk of depression and anxiety (Holt-Lunstad et al. 2010).

+ Studies show that people with strong social ties live longer and experience fewer chronic illnesses than those who are socially isolated (House et al. 1988).

+ Loneliness has been linked to increased levels of cortisol, the stress hormone, which negatively affects health (Cacioppo and Cacioppo 2014).

The neuroscience of connections and emotional regulation

+ Human connection activates the brain's oxytocin system, which promotes trust, reduces stress, and enhances social bonding (Zak 2012).

+ Mirror neurons help individuals develop empathy and emotional understanding, strengthening interpersonal relationships (Iacoboni 2009).

+ Engaging in positive social interactions can lower amygdala hyperactivity, reducing fear and anxiety responses (Davidson and McEwen 2012).

The impact of relationships on learning and performance

+ Social belonging significantly enhances motivation, academic achievement, and engagement in both students and teachers (Walton and Cohen 2011).

+ Collaborative learning environments improve critical thinking and problem-solving skills through peer interaction (Johnson and Johnson 2009).

+ Teachers who develop strong relationships with students report higher levels of job satisfaction and resilience against burnout (Spilt et al. 2011).

The Role of Emotional Intelligence in Building Connections

+ Emotional intelligence (EI) enhances interpersonal relationships, as individuals with high EI navigate social interactions more effectively (Goleman 1995).

+ Higher EI is linked to increased workplace performance, reduced stress levels, and greater leadership effectiveness (Brackett et al. 2011).

The importance of psychological safety in relationships

+ Psychological safety—the belief that one can speak up and take risks without fear of embarrassment—leads to stronger team cohesion and productivity (Edmondson 1999).Positive social environments foster a sense of belonging, reducing feelings of isolation and increasing collaboration (Baumeister and Leary 1995).

- ✦ The power of social support in stress reduction

- ✦ Having strong social support networks buffers against the negative effects of stress and increases resilience (Cohen and Wills 1985).

- ✦ Supportive relationships reduce perceived stress levels and increase one's ability to cope with challenges (Taylor 2011).

The science of reciprocity and relationship-building

- ✦ Reciprocity—the act of giving and receiving—builds trust and strengthens relationships over time (Gouldner 1960).

- ✦ Acts of kindness and gratitude in social interactions increase overall well-being and deepen social bonds (Emmons and McCullough 2003).

MEET THE TEACHER: Real-Life Application

Ms. Migalie started her first year with high hopes and a clear vision of the warm, thriving classroom community she wanted to create. As the weeks passed, that vision felt further and further out of reach.

Her first graders were bright and energetic, but their interactions were anything but harmonious. Friendships were fragile, dissolving over the smallest disagreements. Group work often led to frustration, with some students struggling to collaborate while others hesitated to engage at all. Morning meetings, meant to foster connection, were half-hearted participation and disruptive behavior. Her coursework only touched on classroom management and community building, and she realized that stepping into an already established classroom as a student teacher hadn't prepared her for the everyday challenges of making it all work in her own classroom.

Ms. Migalie found herself feeling defeated. She had expected teaching to be hard, but she hadn't anticipated how lonely and overwhelming it could be when things didn't go as planned. She knew that a sense of belonging was crucial—not just for her students, but for herself. The teachers' lounge was like a dungeon of doom. The relationships she had with her colleagues were superficial at best. She did not feel safe around some of them. How could she foster a culture of belonging in her classroom when she felt so disconnected herself? She knew staying on top of paperwork and delivering instruction would improve over time, but would she figure out the community piece?

A TEACHER'S MEMOIR:
Learning from Others

At the start of the school year, I had a vision of the warm, thriving classroom I wanted to create—one where every child felt important and excited to learn. As the weeks passed, that vision began to slip away. My students often didn't get along, collaborative efforts were a nightmare, and morning meetings felt chaotic. I knew that a sense of belonging was essential, yet I felt I was failing to create it. Worse still, I felt completely alone; even the teachers' lounge felt like a dungeon rather than a sanctuary. I needed a way to reset and turn things around.

I learned from High Five to Thrive that research in psychology, neuroscience, and education tells us that building and maintaining meaningful connections is not just a nice-to-have; it is vital for personal well-being, professional success, and overall life satisfaction. Strong social relationships help improve mental and physical health, regulate stress hormones, and foster trust and empathy through our brain's natural mechanisms. Positive interactions can boost learning, enhance job satisfaction, and even make us more resilient by creating a sense of psychological safety and belonging. In short, meaningful connections transform isolation into collaboration and stress into shared strength.

That's also how I found the Teacher Connection Plan. As I began filling its pages, everything came into perspective. I made discoveries about myself and the way I approached my role as a teacher—and, if I'm honest, life in general. It became my lifeline.

One of the first insights from the journal was that my exhaustion and frustration weren't solely about my students; they were also about me. I had been so focused on taking care of everyone else that I had neglected my own needs. The journal prompted me to think about what I required to feel grounded, so I started a simple mindfulness practice each morning—a few minutes to breathe and reset. Although it wasn't an instant cure, it made a noticeable difference. I entered my classroom with more patience and energy, and an acute awareness of how my well-being influenced the connections I was striving to build.

One reflection asked me to recall a time when building a connection made a difference. I immediately thought of a student who had been struggling socially, emotionally, and academically. Previously, I might not have had the bandwidth to reach out, but with connection at the forefront of my mind, I made the effort. I checked in with her more often, encouraged her, and made sure she felt seen. Slowly, her confidence blossomed, and she began participating more actively. One connection, one small shift, changed everything—for her and for me. It reminded me that even the smallest gesture can have a profound impact, a truth supported by the science of social bonds.

To foster a sense of community, I had to be intentional about creating shared experiences. I introduced new class rituals—starting each day with a brief time to share news, where students could tell personal stories, practice active listening, and show mutual respect. I also implemented a quote journal, writing an inspiring quote on the board each morning for students to reflect upon in their own journals before we discussed them as a group. The change was subtle at first, but soon students who had been hesitant began to speak up, deeper conversations unfolded, and a true sense of community emerged. These small, deliberate actions helped my students discover common ground and appreciate each other's perspectives.

I also began paying closer attention to making everyone feel valued—greeting students by name, asking about their hobbies, celebrating their successes, and showing genuine interest in their lives. I extended that same energy to my colleagues, introducing them to one another with enthusiasm and always seeking ways to uplift them. These small acts, though seemingly minor, had a huge impact—turning a chilly environment into one filled with warmth and connection.

Implementing the Teacher Connection Plan in my classroom has been nothing short of transformative. I discovered that by blending clear expectations with shared experiences, empathetic communication, and purposeful praise, I could create a learning environment where every student felt secure, celebrated, and truly connected. Below, I share my journey along with actionable strategies organized under key sections.

Section 1: Explicitly Teaching Expectations

I still remember the first day I introduced clear, evidence-based expectations to my students. By outlining concrete norms and micro-behaviors, I created an environment where everyone knew what to expect. This clarity reduced anxiety and built a foundation of trust. Over time, I saw my students become more confident and engaged because they felt safe and understood.

Section 2: Win Big with Rich Shared Experiences

Integrating shared experiences into my daily routine changed the classroom dynamics. I started celebrating both small and big wins—not just academic milestones, but moments of kindness, collaboration, and personal growth. These shared celebrations helped build a community where every student felt recognized and connected, boosting both their confidence and academic engagement.

Section 3: Communication and Connections

Changing my communication style was a game-changer. Instead of focusing on corrections, I made a conscious decision to connect. I learned to listen deeply and respond with empathy, even when offering guidance or tough love. This shift not only preserved my students' dignity but also created a more open and trusting classroom atmosphere where mistakes became opportunities for growth.

Section 4: The Power of Praise

I soon discovered that praise could be a secret weapon in building self-esteem and reinforcing positive behavior. Previously, I had mostly focused on rewarding rule-following. By differentiating between effort-based, behavior-based, and noncontingent praise, I was able to recognize each student's unique contributions. This balanced approach not only motivated my students to work harder but also fostered an overall positive and inclusive classroom culture. Now, I make it a point to recognize students for their perseverance, kindness, and unique strengths, not just for compliance. The impact was clear: students who once faded into the background now shined with confidence and enthusiasm.

Section 5: Focus on Common Ground

One of the most rewarding parts of this journey was discovering the power of common ground. By highlighting shared interests and values during lessons, I helped my students see that, despite their differences, they all had something in common. This focus not only reduced conflicts but also built a strong sense of community, where every student felt a part of the collective journey.

Section 6: Connecting Outside the Four Walls of the Classroom

The impact of the Teacher Connection Plan extended far beyond the classroom. At first, I thought my isolation stemmed solely from the people around me, but through the Teacher Connection Plan process, I realized I was contributing to it by not reaching out. I took a small step and contacted a colleague about collaborating on a project. That partnership not only improved our work but also brought fun and companionship into my routine, alleviating my feelings of loneliness. By communicating with warmth and a collaborative spirit, I built networks that enriched not only the academic experience but also the overall support system for my students. The ripple effect was remarkable—stronger home-school relationships, a more engaged Professional Learning Community, and new opportunities for community involvement. I also started viewing interactions with administrators and parents differently—not as tasks to be completed, but as opportunities for genuine connection. Changing my mindset and approach opened the door to unexpected support and camaraderie.

Final Reflection

This entire reflection process changed everything for me. I discovered practical solutions and, more importantly, realized that connection isn't just a nice add-on—it's the foundation of a thriving, safe, and fulfilling environment. Meaningful connections make students feel secure enough to take risks, enable teachers to feel supported, and transform a stressful job into a truly rewarding calling.

I no longer feel like I'm just keeping my head above water. I feel empowered—to care for myself, to nurture relationships, and to build a culture where everyone, both students and teachers, feels valued and included. I love my job! (Well, not every minute, but overall, I truly love teaching!)

Highlights of Ms. Migalie's Experience

Ms. Migalie found clarity and purpose through engaging with the Teacher's Wellness Connection Plan. This experience empowered her to see herself as a connector, not just an educator—transforming her classroom and reigniting her passion for teaching. Below are the key highlights of what she learned:

The role of social connections in mental and physical health

+ Ms. Migalie realized that prioritizing relationships led to a positive shift in her classroom, improving engagement and support. Research confirms that strong social ties enhance mental health and reduce stress through the brain's oxytocin system (House et al. 1988; Cacioppo and Cacioppo 2014; Zak 2012).

The neuroscience of connections and emotional regulation

+ Ms. Migalie found that mindfulness and self-care improved her emotional regulation, enabling her to form healthier relationships with students and colleagues. Research highlights that mindfulness practices lower stress and enhance emotional stability, making social connections stronger (Kabat-Zinn 1990; Goyal et al. 2014; Holt-Lunstad et al. 2010).

The impact of relationships on learning and performance

+ By implementing classroom rituals and collaborative projects, Ms. Migalie fostered a strong sense of belonging and teamwork. Studies show that collaborative environments boost academic engagement, critical thinking, and problem-solving skills (Walton and Cohen 2011; Johnson and Johnson 2009).

The role of emotional intelligence in building connections

+ Shifting from correction to connection, Ms. Migalie strengthened relationships with her students by addressing their emotions with empathy. Emotional intelligence research supports that empathy enhances interpersonal bonds, creating a more supportive learning environment (Goleman 1995; Iacoboni 2009).

The importance of psychological safety in relationships

+ Ms. Migalie realized the importance of collaboration beyond the classroom, strengthening relationships with colleagues, administrators, and parents. Research confirms that psychological safety fosters teamwork and prevents isolation, benefiting educators and students alike (Edmondson 1999; Baumeister and Leary 1995).

The power of social support in stress reduction

+ Through reflection, Ms. Migalie saw that reciprocity, kindness, and gratitude strengthened her social bonds and well-being. Studies highlight that supportive relationships buffer stress and improve resilience (Cohen and Wills 1985; Taylor 2011).

The science of reciprocity and relationship-building

+ Ms. Migalie learned to use balanced praise to reinforce student success and build a positive classroom culture. Research confirms that varied praise techniques enhance engagement, reduce behavioral issues, and foster resilience (Emmons and McCullough 2003; Waldinger and Schultz 2023).

YOUR TURN:
Take Action for Traction

To get the most out of this Teacher Connection Plan, follow these steps with intention and focus. This process is designed to help you identify "small biggies"—those small yet powerful shifts that can create a significant impact on your well-being and teaching experience.

+ Find a quiet, comfortable place where you can think and reflect without distractions.

+ Bring a notebook, journal, or digital device to capture your thoughts.

+ Take a few deep breaths to center yourself and approach this with an open mind.

Directions for Completing the Teacher Connection Plan

1. **Familiarize yourself with the plan.** Read through the six sections of the Teacher Connection Plan. Understanding the rationale behind each section will help you see how these strategies create a positive, research-based learning environment (Marzano 2003; Durlak et al. 2011).

   » Explicitly Teach Expectations

   » Win Big with Rich Shared Experiences

   » Communicate to Connect

   » The Power of Praise

   » Focus on Common Ground

   » Connecting Outside the Four Walls of Your Classroom

2. **Reflect on your current practices.** For each section, take a moment to reflect on how your current classroom practices align with these strategies. Use the Reflection column in the provided tables to note your thoughts. Ask yourself the following questions:

    »   What is working well in my classroom?

    »   Where do I see room for growth in building connections?

3. **Identify concrete action steps.** In the Action Step column, determine specific steps you can take to address the reflections. For example, if you notice that your class routines need more structure, decide on clear, evidence-based norms to implement. This step is crucial because research shows that explicitly teaching expectations reduces anxiety and builds trust (Pianta 2006).

4. **Develop a detailed action plan.** In the Action Plan column, outline measurable, time-bound tasks that will help you implement your action steps. These plans will provide you with a roadmap for fostering a classroom environment where every student feels secure and valued. Consider the following:

    »   Daily or weekly routines

    »   Specific activities or rituals

    »   Methods for tracking progress and adjusting practices

5. **Integrate strategies into your daily routine.** Begin applying the new strategies in your classroom. Research indicates that these practices lead to improved student engagement and a positive classroom climate (Rogers 1961; Waldinger and Schultz 2023). For instance:

    »   Clearly articulate and model classroom expectations every day.

    »   Incorporate shared experiences into lesson plans to celebrate small and big wins.

    »   Use empathetic language that focuses on connection rather than correction.

6. **Monitor your progress.** Regularly revisit your tables to update your reflections, adjust your action steps, and refine your action plan. Tracking progress will help you see the impact of your efforts on classroom behavior and student engagement.

7. **Collaborate with others.** Extend these connection strategies beyond your classroom by engaging with colleagues, parents, and community partners. Sharing your experiences and insights can lead to a broader support network that enriches the learning environment (Epstein 2018).

8. **Evaluate and celebrate success.** After implementing the plan for a set period, evaluate the changes in your classroom. Celebrate improvements in student behavior, engagement, and the overall classroom climate. This reflection and celebration phase reinforces the science behind these practices—creating environments where every student can thrive.

Scan to Unlock Bonus Content (Teacher Connection Plan)

By following these directions, you'll be able to systematically implement the Teacher Connection Plan, turning proven-backed strategies into practical actions that transform your classroom. Enjoy the journey toward creating a more connected, inspiring, and supportive learning environment!

JOURNALING:
Reflect and Bloom

Scan to Unlock Bonus Content (Journaling-Reflect and Bloom)

REMEMBER, this page is for you to write down your feelings, struggles, successes, anything you feel you need or want to process after reading this chapter. If you are not accustomed to journaling, you can:

1. **Start with a prompt.** If you're unsure where to begin, you can use these guided prompts:

   » How have your relationships with your students grown or deepened?

» In what ways has your sense of connection with a supportive community of educators changed?

» What actions will you take to continue strengthening and sustaining meaningful relationships in your personal and professional life?

2. **Write freely and honestly.** Don't worry about grammar or structure. This is your space to express yourself openly.

3. **Make it your own.** Customize your journaling practice with doodles, pictures, bullet points, creative storytelling, or any format that helps you reflect and connect with your journey.

Take a deep breath, let your thoughts flow, and allow this space to support your growth and transformation.

COACHING QUESTIONS:
Sustain Growth

As a reminder:

Scan to Unlock Bonus Content (Coaching Questions-Sustain Growth)

+ **Write** down questions you still have about the content, yourself, your feelings, emotions, etc.

+ **Discuss** questions in small groups, in a book study, or with a friend.

+ **Email** Best Questers with your questions at any time (info@bestquesters.net).

+ **Discuss** in coaching conversations in professional learning communities or working with a mentor to facilitate productive discussions and support.

Conclusion

Reflecting on Your Growth

Congratulations on reaching the final chapter of this book—even though in many ways, this is just the beginning. The journey to thriving isn't a one-time event. It's an ongoing process of growth, renewal, and empowerment. You have worked the practices of the The Best Questers High Five to Thrive Formula™ and utilized the tools for each practice to feel more connected to your "why"; foster a more thriving mindset and belief in possibilities; transformed our thoughts and self-talk that shape our self-belief and how we handle life; cultivated mind-body harmony by prioritizing well-being without guilt; and, solidified connections by building relationships that uplift and sustain you. Ultimately, by building the five practices of the The Best Questers High Five to Thrive Formula™, you started experiencing a more thriving state of being. You have taken real, actionable steps to reclaim joy, balance, and impact as an educator.

We know there is a desperate need for educators to find calm in chaos because "without peace in our storm, we feel stuck" (Leaf 2021). We know that we function better mentally and physically when we have peace. You now have some new perspectives and tools, and you have had opportunities to decide what ideas best suit your unique personality and circumstances. You have worked through exercises to synthesize and apply your small biggies. How is this landing for you?

Thinking about peace can shift our perception and even change the chemistry and structure of our brain and body. The more we think about something like this, the more likely it is that we will act on it.

To add, please remember that peace doesn't equal happiness. Being at peace doesn't mean the chaos around you will end and you will be happy. You might need to find some time to breathe when you're caught up in the "quicksand" of life.

Meanwhile, be kind to yourself. When things get tough, be patient and show yourself some self-compassion. Chaos is part of life, but it doesn't have to ruin you (Leaf 2021).

Revisiting Your Commitment

At the start of this journey, you wrote a Sample Commitment Statement—a promise to yourself to engage fully in this process. Take a moment to reflect on your growth:

+ What helped you stick to your commitment?

+ What challenges or obstacles got you off track?

+ What strategy or habit helped you the most?

+ Would you go through this process again? Why or why not?

Use the Recommitment Statement in the Bonus Content to jot down your reflections.

Scan to Unlock Bonus Content (Reflection on My Commitment)

Refining Your Commitment – Your Next Step Forward

Reflect on your progress. You started this journey with a commitment to reduce stress, embrace new ideas, and step out of your comfort zone—and now, you've gained the tools to make it happen.

Now it's time to refine and strengthen your commitment. Think about the strategies that have made the biggest impact on you. What habits do you want to keep? How will you continue prioritizing your well-being while empowering your students?

Write your new commitment statement in the space below, using the present tense to affirm your growth and determination. Let this be your personal reminder—a declaration of how you're moving forward with clarity, confidence, and purpose. You're not the same person who started this book. You've learned, grown, and taken action. Now, let's put it into words and own this next chapter of your journey. You've got this!

Use the space below to write your new commitment statement: My Commitment Statement:

Post-Assessment: How Far Have You Come?

Now that you've put the Best Questers High Five to Thrive Formula™ into practice, let's measure your growth and progress by revisiting the assessment from the beginning of the book. This self-assessment will help you reflect on the growth you've experienced and identify areas where you can continue to strengthen your well-being, effectiveness, and fulfillment as an educator.

This pre/post self-assessment is designed to help you reflect on where you currently stand in key areas that impact your well-being and effectiveness as an educator. The bar graph will help you visualize your strengths and areas for growth across five core categories.

Steps to Complete the Assessment

1 **Answer** Truthfully – Read each question carefully and rate yourself on a scale from 1 to 4:

1 = Not at all

2 = Somewhat

3 = A good amount

4 = Extremely so

2 **Calculate Your Score** – Each category has two related questions. Add your two ratings together for each category.

3 **Find the Average** – Since each category has two questions, divide the total by 2 to find your average score for that area.

4 **Plot Your Results** – Take your averaged score for each category and mark it on the bar graph.

5   **Reflect on Your Results** – Look at your graph to identify areas of strength and opportunities for growth. Use the tools in this book to enhance your well-being in areas where your scores are lower.

Example Calculation:

If you rated yourself a 3 and a 4 in the "Feeling connected to your 'why'" category:

(3 + 4) ÷ 2 = 3.5

Plot 3.5 on the graph in the corresponding row.

This visual representation can help you track your progress over time as you implement new tools for growth and resilience.

Questions

Record your ratings by writing down the rating for each question.

Purpose – Feeling connected to your "why"	
How clear is your sense of purpose and meaning in your work as an educator?	Rating
Do you have defined goals for the impact you want to make in your students' lives?	Rating
Hope – A thriving mindset and belief in possibilities	
How hopeful and optimistic do you feel about your future in education?	Rating
When challenges arise, how often do you feel confident in your ability to stay solution-focused and resilient?	Rating
Mindset – The thoughts and self-talk that shape your self-belief and how you handle life	
How often is your internal dialogue positive and encouraging?	Rating
Do you actively try to shift negative self-talk to a more supportive mindset?	Rating
Mind-Body Harmony – Prioritizing well-being without guilt	
How often do you engage in self-care practices that support your mental and physical well-being?	Rating
Do you feel in control (or not in control) of your emotional and physical wellness, especially in stressful situations?	Rating

Connections – Building relationships that uplift and sustain you	
How strong are your relationships with your students?	Rating
How connected do you feel to a supportive community of educators?	Rating

Input Your Ratings into the Bar Graph

Plot each rating on the horizontal axis next to the corresponding question on the vertical axis

Post-Assessment Scores by Strategy

High Five to Thrive Pre- and Post- Assessment Scoring Rubric

This is the rubric with clear descriptors for each of the five practices, scored on a 1–4 scale, to guide reflection and progress.

Practices	1-Beginning	2-Exploring	3-Developing	4-Thriving
Purpose Feeling connected to your "why"	Completely disconnected from purpose; lacks motivation and passion.	Has moments of passion and engagement but lacks consistency.	Regularly connects with purpose and finds meaning in teaching.	Fully embodies and lives their purpose daily, inspiring and leading others.
Hope A thriving mindset and belief in possibilities	Feels stuck and overwhelmed by problems. Struggles to see possibilities. Primarily focuses on obstacles and lacks confidence in overcoming them	Is beginning to reframe challenges into opportunities and explore solutions. Takes small steps toward positive problem-solving but still experiences self-doubt.	Uses hopeful thinking to navigate difficulties and actively looks for solutions. Demonstrates resilience and begins to apply tools to shift focus from obstacles to opportunities.	Naturally turns obstacles into opportunities and thrives in uncertainty. Fully embraces a growth mindset, confidently taking action to create solutions and inspire hope in others.
Mindset The thoughts and self-talk that shape your self-belief and how you handle life	Negative self-talk dominates, leading to self-doubt and discouragement. Struggles to recognize or challenge negative thoughts.	Uses some positive self-talk tools but inconsistently. Has moments of confidence but still struggles with self-doubt in challenging situations.	Applies positive self-talk regularly to boost confidence and resilience. Actively works to reframe negative thoughts and maintain a balanced mindset.	Mastery of self-talk, with automatic positive thought patterns that uplift and empower. Inspires and mentors others in developing a resilient and confident mindset.

Practices	1-Beginning	2-Exploring	3-Developing	4-Thriving
Mind-Body Harmony Prioritizing well-being without guilt	Experiences extreme stress, exhaustion, and burnout. No self-care or well-being tools in place, leading to emotional and physical strain.	Implements some stress management techniques but inconsistently. Begins to prioritize self-care but still experiences frequent burnout.	Engages in self-care and stress regulation with reasonable consistency. Has tools in place to maintain energy and manage emotions.	Fully integrates well-being into daily life, effortlessly balancing stress and energy. Thrives in a state of calm, focus, and resilience, inspiring others to do the same.
Connections Building relationships that uplift and sustain you	Feels isolated and disconnected from colleagues, students, or the school community. Avoids collaboration and struggles to engage in meaningful interactions.	Actively working on building relationships and collaboration. Finds value in connecting with others but still struggles with consistency or depth.	Builds and maintains meaningful connections with colleagues and students. Engages in collaboration and communication regularly, fostering a positive environment.	Thrives in a network of deep, lasting, and positive connections that uplift all. Acts as a connector, fostering a strong sense of community and belonging.

Scoring Interpretation:

- 🖐 5–8: **Beginning:** Don't be discouraged—this score shows where you are now, not where you'll stay. Keep using the five strategies and tools in the book, and you'll continue growing with every step forward.

- 🖐 9–12: **Exploring:** You have some pieces in place. Focus on refining your approach to strengthen your impact and satisfaction.

- 🖐 13–16: **Developing:** You're well on your way! Keep applying these tools to thrive in your teaching and well-being.

- 🖐 17–20: **Thriving:** You are thriving! Add new or strengthen your practices to sustain growth and inspire others.

This post-assessment will help you recognize your growth and identify the next steps on your journey. Keep thriving!

Scan to Unlock Bonus Content (Reflecting on Results)

Reflecting on Results

- ✦ Compare your scores to your initial assessment.

- ✦ What has changed?

- ✦ Where have you seen the biggest improvement?

- ✦ What areas still need focus?

- ✦ Take a moment to celebrate your progress—every step, no matter how small, contributes to lasting growth. As you reflect on your answers, identify one key takeaway and one action step that will help you continue thriving in your life and work. What's your next move?

No matter where your scores **land**, this process isn't about perfection—it's about progress. In fact, we have taken the word "perfect" out of our vocabulary! LOL!

Throughout this book, we addressed some of the most pressing challenges educators face today:

- ✦ **Loss of purpose** – You connected to your "why" and aligned your daily work with your deeper mission.

- ✦ **Feeling of hopelessness** – You learned how to shift your mindset from frustration to possibility, using hope as a strategy.

- ✦ **Unhelpful mindset patterns** – You flipped the script from unhelpful thought patterns and self-talk to empowering thoughts and self-talk.

- ✦ **Overlooking mind-body harmony** – You developed tools to help you improve your mind-body harmony enhancing your overall well-being.

- ✦ **Feeling disconnected** – You explored how strengthening meaningful relationships with students, colleagues, and mentors fuel resilience and professional fulfillment.

Moving Forward: Keep Growing, Keep Thriving

The journey doesn't end here. Real transformation happens when you keep practicing the tools you've learned and continue taking small, intentional steps forward. Here's how you can keep your progress going:

- ✦ **Revisit the Best Questers' High Five to Thrive Formula™ regularly.** Use this framework whenever you feel stuck or overwhelmed. It's your roadmap to resilience.

- ✦ **Commit to ongoing reflection and journaling.** Regularly revisit the coaching questions and journal prompts to track your growth.

- ✦ **Lean on your Hope Agents,** Surround yourself with colleagues, mentors, and friends who uplift and encourage you.

- ✦ **Use hope stacking and hope habits to stay motivated.** Celebrate even the smallest victories, because every step forward is progress.

- ✦ **Pass it on.** Share what you've learned with others who need encouragement. Becoming a Hope Agent for others keeps hope alive in you, too.

MEET THE TEACHER:
See Real-Life Applications

Ms. Dobbs had always loved teaching, but lately, the job felt like too much.

As a high school teacher of English language learners, she was used to challenges—students arriving mid-year with little to no English, navigating cultural differences, advocating for their needs, and helping them prepare for graduation. Lately, the stress has become overwhelming.

Her desk was buried under a mountain of assignments needing feedback, yet grading wasn't the hardest part. Many of her students faced struggles beyond the classroom—language barriers, financial stress, immigration concerns, and pressure to succeed in a new country. How could she possibly help them all? The weight of their challenges sat heavily on her shoulders, and the joy she once felt in the classroom seemed to be slipping away.

Each morning, she forced herself to walk through the school doors, exhausted before the day even began. Even her students, typically resilient and eager to learn, seemed to sense her struggle. She knew they needed her energy, her encouragement—but how could she give what she no longer felt herself?

Then, one day, a colleague introduced her to *High Five to Thrive*, a program designed to help teachers reconnect with their purpose and find hope in the midst of exhaustion.

Ms. Dobbs was skeptical. Another professional development program? Could a book and a workshop really make a difference when she felt this lost? *I mean, don't we already have enough training sessions that never actually help?*

But with nothing to lose, she decided to give it a try.

A TEACHER'S MEMOIR:
Learn from Others

When I first picked up High Five to Thrive, *I wasn't expecting much. I was just trying to get through each day, feeling overwhelmed and exhausted. But something about the Best Questers High Five to Thrive Formula, Purpose + Hope + Mindset + Mind-Body Harmony + Connections = Thriving, stuck with me. It reminded me that knowing wasn't enough. I had to do something.*

Practice 1: Purpose *was a game-changer. Teaching had once been my passion, but the daily grind had buried that spark. This chapter pushed me to reflect on why I started teaching in the first place. I started a simple hope habit each morning—writing* *down one happy classroom moment from the day before. At first, it felt like any other task, but I'm glad I kept at it because it definitely upgraded my daily reality! In time I noticed that the more I looked for positive moments, the more I saw them. This tiny habit planted seeds of gratitude that grew into a renewed sense of purpose.*

***Practice 2: Hope** taught me to reframe challenges. Before, classroom struggles felt like walls I couldn't break through. But this chapter taught me to reframe those obstacles as opportunities for growth and creativity. One student, Ghandi, was especially disruptive, and I took it personally. But instead of seeing his behavior as a problem, I got curious. I started focusing on him instead of the disruptions. I made a point to talk with him, setting small, manageable goals and celebrating every success. The progress was slow, but it came. His engagement grew, and so did my belief in the power of small, intentional efforts.*

I realized that problem behaviors are an invitation to try something different. I wasn't just managing his disruptions; I was helping him build confidence and find his own motivation. Instead of feeling stuck, I felt empowered to make a difference. Harnessing Hope didn't just change how I approached problems; it renewed my belief in the potential for positive change, in both my students and myself.

***Practice 3: Mindset** opened my eyes to how my own self-talk was holding me back. I'd been carrying a constant loop of doubt: "I'm not good enough," "I'll never get this right." This chapter helped me see that those thoughts weren't facts; they were just stories that were keeping me stuck. My self-talk had been hacking away at my hope. The tools in Flipping the Script gave me a way to rewrite that internal narrative. I started replacing them with hope-filled truths. Slowly, those new thoughts took root, and I felt stronger. My confidence grew, not just as a teacher, but as a person.*

Flipping the Script wasn't just about changing my thoughts; it was about changing my relationship with myself. The impact has been huge, in my teaching and in my personal life too.

***Practice 4: Mind-Body Harmony** taught me how to stay grounded in tough moments. Before, when there was a behavior problem or the pressure of looming deadlines was getting to me, I reacted on autopilot. My body would tense up, my thoughts would spiral, and I'd react without thinking, adding to the chaos. I started using tools from the Cool Calm Kit, such as deep breathing and grounding exercises. At first, it seemed too simple to work, but over time, it changed everything.*

One of the first things I implemented was deep breathing exercises using one of the breathing cards to guide me. I placed other tools, such as stress balls and affirmations, around the room. One of my favorite techniques is using grounding exercises from the kit; whenever I feel my stress rising, I pause to focus on the feeling of the stress ball in my hand to bring my attention back to the present moment. These small habits help me reset my emotions and approach situations with a clearer, calmer mindset.

My students picked up on my calmer energy, and the whole classroom atmosphere has become more peaceful. I feel more in control, and my students are more on track. I feel like I'm no longer reacting; I respond with intention.

***Practice 5: Connections** brought me back to a fundamental truth: connection is everything. I made a conscious effort to build stronger relationships—with students, colleagues, and parents. I made time for one-on-one conversations, where they could share their thoughts and feelings. It wasn't always easy to find that time, but the impact has been incredible!*

One of my favorite changes was starting a Hope Jar. Students wrote down small wins, things they were proud of, or hopes for the future. In tough moments, we pull out a note and read it aloud, reminding ourselves of the progress we were making. I noticed that we supported each other more and celebrated with each other.

Leaning into the Praise Pack as a starting point to build an environment of unconditional positive regard has turned out to be powerful. Students feel valued not just for what they accomplish but for who they are. Students who had been disengaged have started to open up, and the overall dynamic in the classroom is more positive and supportive.

I also extended this effort to my relationships with colleagues and parents. With colleagues, I prioritized collaboration, turning to them not just for support but as hope agents who reinforced my growth. This has strengthened our professional connections and created a stronger support network. With parents, I reach out more—not just to discuss problems but to celebrate wins, strengthening our partnership. Prioritizing connection was transformative for me and for my students, and it's made a huge difference in all my relationships.

Now that I've completed this part of my journey, I feel like a completely different person. I hardly recognize the overwhelmed, exhausted teacher I once was. I'm more connected—to my students, colleagues, and parents, and profession. But just as importantly, I've reconnected with my own purpose and sense of self. I'm no longer feeling lost in the chaos; instead, I'm centered, confident, and at peace. I know how to manage the stresses that come with teaching, and I've created a sustainable practice that allows me to stay balanced, even on the toughest days. I'm not just surviving—I'm thriving, and my students are, too!

I'm so incredibly grateful for this experience. High Five to Thrive *has given me the tools I needed to turn my teaching career—and my life— around. And the best part is, I know this isn't just a temporary change. The hope habits and mindsets I've developed will continue to support me and my students for years to come.*

Highlights of Ms. Dobb's Experience

Ms. Dobbs experienced thriving by working through the elements of the Best Questers High Five to Thrive Formula™ and making intentional choices to apply the five practices. She emerged feeling empowered, hopeful, and deeply connected to her students and my teaching career. Here are the key highlights of what she learned:

Purpose. Ms. Dobbs reconnected with her "why" for teaching by reflecting on meaningful classroom moments and cultivating a daily gratitude practice. This simple habit reignited her passion and enhanced her sense of purpose, supporting emotional well-being and resilience (Emmons and McCullough 2003; Fredrickson 2009).

Hope. By reframing challenges as opportunities, Ms. Dobbs developed a daily hope habit that transformed obstacles into moments of growth and creativity. This shift in perspective fostered optimism and empowered her to support student development, in line with hope theory's emphasis on goal-directed thinking (Snyder 2002).

Mindset. Through the Flipping the Script process, Ms. Dobbs transformed her negative self-talk into hope-filled truths. This cognitive shift not only boosted her confidence but also enhanced her overall resilience, reflecting core principles of cognitive behavioral therapy (Beck 1976; Burns 1980).

Mind-Body Harmony. Utilizing tools from the Cool Calm Kit—such as deep breathing exercises and grounding techniques—Ms. Dobbs learned to manage stress effectively and maintain emotional control. These mindfulness practices helped her shift from reactive to responsive behavior, promoting a calm and focused classroom environment (Kabat-Zinn 1990; Jerath et al. 2006).

Connections. By intentionally building relationships with students, colleagues, and parents—through initiatives such as the Hope Jar and the Praise Pack—Ms. Dobbs created a more positive and supportive classroom culture. Strengthening these social bonds improved communication, increased engagement, and fostered a strong sense of community, which is essential for mental and emotional health (Holt-Lunstad et al. 2010; House et al. 1988).

Weaving It All Together

Ms. Dobbs' story in Chapter 5 wasn't just about her; it was about you and every educator navigating the complexities of teaching. Her journey was a reflection of the real challenges educators face and, more importantly, the real transformation that is possible when tools are put into action.

By reflecting on her journey, you were able to see the reality of implementing these practices—not in a perfect, linear way, but in a way that adapts to real-life struggles. Ms. Dobbs showed that thriving isn't about eliminating challenges; it's about equipping yourself to navigate through them.

Her story was important because it demonstrated that growth is a choice. She didn't wait for the perfect circumstances or for someone else to change her environment. Instead, she took ownership by working through the five practices. She proved that small, consistent actions lead to lasting change.

Why was it important for you to read her story? Because her success is a testament to what's possible for you, too. She started where you might have started—uncertain, exhausted, and searching for change—but she ended up thriving, not because her circumstances magically improved, but because she made the choice to apply the tools and commit to her growth.

Now, it's your turn. How will you take what you've learned and put it into action? Like Ms. Dobbs, you have the practices and the tools. Now, it's about using them to shape a future where you, too, can thrive. Your journey starts now.

Final Words: Your Commitment to Thriving

As we reach the end of this part of our journey together, we want to express how much we've enjoyed sharing the lessons, insights, and experiences we've gathered over the years. It has been an honor to walk alongside you as you navigate this path, and we sincerely hope that these ideas resonate with you and help you bring about the changes you desire in your life and in the lives of your students.

Thank you for allowing us to be a part of your journey. We wish you nothing but the very best as you move forward with confidence, hope, and renewed energy. May your work bring light and joy to your students, and may you continue to grow and thrive in all that you do.

We would love to hear from you. Your stories, your successes, and even your challenges are important to us, and we welcome the opportunity to continue this conversation. Please know that we are rooting for you, and we believe in the incredible potential that lies ahead. We are eager to hear great testimonies from you!

You were meant for more.
Thrive forward!

Donita, Viki & Debbie
The Best Quester's Team

Please contact us at info@bestquesters.net

References Cited

Baker, J. "The Effects of Fidget Tools on Classroom Focus and Stress Reduction." *Journal of Behavioral Education* 27, no. 4 (2018): 523-539. https://doi.org/10.1007/s10864-018-9285-1.

Barton, John, Lisa M. Reynolds, and Mark A. Carter. *The Power of Positive Reflection in Workplace Well-Being.* Cambridge University Press, 2023.

Barton, J., Bragg, R., Wood, C., & Pretty, J. (2023). "The Psychological and Emotional Benefits of Gratitude Writing in Workplace Settings." *Journal of Occupational Health Psychology* 28, no. 3: 421-437. https://doi.org/10.1037/ocp0000347.

Baumeister, Rcy F., and Mark R. Leary. "The Need to Belong: Desire for Interpersonal Attachments as a Fundamental Human Motivation." *Psychological Bulletin* 117, no. 3 (1995): 497-529. https://doi.org/10.1037/0033-2909.117.3.497.

Beck, Aaron T. *Cognitive Therapy and the Emotional Disorders.* International Universities Press, 1976.

Ben-Shahar, T. (2007). *Learn to be Happier. Week by Week.* Journal.

Brackett, Marc A., Susan E. Rivers, and Peter Salovey. "Emotional Intelligence: Implications for Personal, Social, Academic, and Workplace Success." *Social and Personality Psychology Compass* 5, no. 1 (2011): 88-103. https://doi.org/10.1111/j.1751-9004.2010.00334.x.

Brown, Richard P., and Patricia L. Gerbarg. "The Healing Power of the Breath." *Journal of Alternative and Complementary Medicine* 18, no. 10 (2012): 879-890. https://doi.org/10.1089/acm.2012.0205.

Burns, David D. *Feeling Good: The New Mood Therapy.* William Morrow, 1980.

Cacioppo, John T., and Stephanie Cacioppo. "Social Relationships and Health: The Toxic Effects of Perceived Social Isolation." Social and Personality Psychology *Baker, J. 2018. "The Effects of Fidget Tools on Classroom Focus and Stress Reduction." Journal of Behavioral Education 27 (4): 523–539. https://doi.org/10.1007/s10864-018-9285-1.*

CASE (Collaborative for Academic, Social, and Emotional Learning). 2020. "What Is SEL?" https://casel.org/what-is-sel/.

Chan, D. W. (2011). Burnout and life satisfaction: Does gratitude intervention make a difference among Chinese school teachers in Hong Kong? Educational Psychology, 31(7), 809-823. https://doi.org/10.1080/01443410.2011.608525

Cheavens, Jennifer S., David B. Feldman, Angela Gum, Shannon T. Michael, and C. R. Snyder. 2005. "Hope Therapy in a Community Sample: A Pilot Investigation." *Social Indicators Research 77 (1): 61–78. https://doi.org/10.1007/s11205-005-5553-0.*

Clear, James. *Atomic Habits: An Easy & Proven Way to Build Good Habits & Break Bad Ones. New York: Avery, 2018.*

Cohen, Geoffrey L. *Belonging: The Science of Creating Connection and Bridging Divides. 2022.*

Cohen, Sheldon, and Thomas A. Wills. 1985. "Stress, Social Support, and the Buffering Hypothesis." *Psychological Bulletin 98 (2): 310–357. https://doi.org/10.1037/0033-2909.98.2.310.*

Cole, M. 2022. *"4 Ways to Intentionally Win with People."* Maxwell Leadership Team Community, *March 1, 2022. Retrieved February 25, 2025. https://www.maxwellleadership.com/blog/4-ways-to-intentionally-win-with-people/*

Corliss, Julia Candace, PhD, and Aaron Dahlgren, PhD. *Unconditional Positive Regard: The Science, Psychology, and Strategies Behind High Performing Classrooms.* Center for Teacher Effectiveness, [2018].

Dahlgren, Rick, and Judy Hyatt. *Time to Teach: Encouragement, Empowerment, and Excellence in Every Classroom.* Center for Teacher Effectiveness, [2007].

Dahlgren, Rich, with Melanie Lattimer. *Teach-To's: 100 Behavior Lesson Plans and Essential Advice to Encourage High Expectations and Winning Classroom Behavior.* Center for Teacher Effectiveness, [2012].

Dahlgren, Rich, Brett Malas, Joanna Faulk, PhD, and Melanie Lattimer. *Time to Teach! The Source for Classroom Management.* Center for Teacher Effectiveness, [2022].

Dana, Deb. 2018. *The Polyvagal Theory in Therapy: Engaging the Rhythm of Regulation. New York: Norton.*

Davidson, Richard J., and Bruce S. McEwen. 2012. "Social Influences on Neuroplasticity: Stress and Interventions to Promote Well-Being." *Nature Neuroscience 15 (5): 689–695. https://doi.org/10.1038/nn.3093.*

Doidge, Norman. 2007. *The Brain That Changes Itself: Stories of Personal Triumph from the Frontiers of Brain Science. New York: Viking.*

Duhigg, Charles. 2012. *The Power of Habit: Why We Do What We Do in Life and Business. New York: Random House.*

Durlak, Joseph A., Roger P. Weissberg, Allison B. Dymnicki, Rebecca D. Taylor, and Kriston B. Schellinger. 2011. *"The Impact of Enhancing Students' Social and*

Emotional Learning: A Meta-Analysis of School-Based Universal Interventions." *Child Development* 82 (1): 405–432.

Edmondson, Amy. 1999. "Psychological Safety and Learning Behavior in Work Teams." *Administrative Science Quarterly 44 (2): 350–383*. https://doi.org/10.2307/2666999.

Emmons, Robert A., Michael E. McCullough, and Jo-Ann Tsang. "The Role of Gratitude in Psychological and Physical Well-Being." *Journal of Personality and Social Psychology* 84, no. 2 (2023): 377-389. https://doi.org/10.1037/0022-3514.84.2.377.

Emmons, R. A., & Mishra, A. (2021). "The Role of Gratitude in Promoting Employee Well-Being and Job Satisfaction." *Applied Psychology: Health and Well-Being* 13, no. 2: 312–329. https://doi.org/10.1111/aphw.12232.

Epstein, Joyce L. *School, Family, and Community Partnerships: Preparing Educators and Improving Schools*. 2nd ed. Westview Press, 2018.

Fogg, B. J. 2019. *Tiny Habits: The Small Changes That Change Everything*. Boston: Houghton Mifflin Harcourt.

Fredrickson, Barbara L. 2009. *Positivity: Top-Notch Research Reveals the 3-to-1 Ratio That Will Change Your Life*. New York: Crown Publishers.

Gallagher, Matthew W., and Shane J. Lopez. 2009. "Positive Expectancies and Mental Health: Identifying the Unique Contributions of Hope and Optimism." *The Journal of Positive Psychology* 4 (6): 548–556.

https://doi.org/10.1080/17439760903157166.

Goleman, Daniel. 1995. *Emotional Intelligence: Why It Can Matter More Than IQ*. New York: Bantam Books.

Gouldner, Alvin W. 1960. "The Norm of Reciprocity: A Preliminary Statement." *American Sociological Review* 25 (2): 161–178. https://doi.org/10.2307/2092623.

Goyal, Madhav, Sonal Singh, Erica M. Sibinga, and Neil F. Gould. 2014. "Meditation Programs for Psychological Stress and Well-Being: A Systematic Review and Meta-Analysis." *JAMA Internal Medicine* 174 (3): 357–368. https://doi.org/10.1001/jamainternmed.2013.13018.

Grandin, Temple. 1992. "Calming Effects of Deep Pressure in Persons with Autism and Other Conditions." *Journal of Child and Adolescent Psychopharmacology* 2 (1): 63–72.

Holt-Lunstad, Julianne, Timothy B. Smith, and J. Bradley Layton. 2010. "Social Relationships and Mortality Risk: A Meta-Analytic Review." *PLoS Medicine* 7 (7): e1000316. https://doi.org/10.1371/journal.pmed.1000316.

House, James S., Karl R. Landis, and Debra Umberson. 1988. "Social Relationships and Health." *Science* 241 (4865): 540–545. https://doi.org/10.1126/science.3399889.

Howard, S., and D. Hughes. 2016. "The Impact of Sensory-Based Interventions on Students' Focus and Stress Levels in the Classroom." *Journal of School Psychology* 58 (3): 45–58. https://doi.org/10.1016/j.jsp.2016.06.004.

Iacoboni, Marco. 2009. *Mirroring People: The New Science of How We Connect with Others.* New York: Farrar, Straus, and Giroux.

Jerath, Ravinder, Jonathan W. Edry, Victor A. Barnes, and Vandna Jerath. 2006. "Physiology of Long Pranayamic Breathing: Neural, Respiratory, and Cardiovascular Correlates." *Medical Hypotheses* 67 (3): 566–571. https://doi.org/10.1016/j.mehy.2006.02.042.

Johnson, David W., and Roger T. Johnson. 2009. "An Educational Psychology Success Story: Social Interdependence Theory and Cooperative Learning." *Educational Researcher* 38 (5): 365–379. https://doi.org/10.3102/0013189X09339057.

Kabat-Zinn, Jon. 1990. *Full Catastrophe Living: Using the Wisdom of Your Body and Mind to Face Stress, Pain, and Illness.* New York: Random House.

Koulivand, Peir Hossein, Giti Khaleghi, and Pouran Mikaili. 2013. "Lavender and the Nervous System." *Evidence-Based Complementary and Alternative Medicine* 2013: 681304. https://doi.org/10.1155/2013/681304.

Krashen, Stephen D. *The Input Hypothesis: Issues and Implications.* Longman, 1985.

Leaf, Caroline. 2021. *Cleaning Up Your Mental Mess: 5 Simple, Scientifically Proven Steps to Reduce Anxiety, Stress, and Toxic Thinking.* Grand Rapids, MI: Baker Books.

Liu, Wenjing, Huili Liu, Ziyu Wang, Yimin Zhang, and Hao Zhao. 2023. "Exploring the Implications of Attention Restoration Theory (ART) in Restorative Environment Design: A Systematic Review." *Sustainability* 16 (9): 3639. https://doi.org/10.3390/su16093639.

Li, Xiao, Hannah K. Weiss, and George F. Bonanno. 2022. "Gratitude and Positive Reframing: Keys to Resilience in the Workplace." *Journal of Occupational Health Psychology* 27 (3): 198–210. https://doi.org/10.1037/ocp0000302.

Marzano, Robert J. 2003. *Classroom Management That Works: Research-Based Strategies for Every Teacher.* Alexandria, VA: ASCD.

Maxwell, John C. 2007. *The 21 Irrefutable Laws of Leadership: Follow Them and People Will Follow You.* 10th Anniversary Edition. Nashville, TN: Thomas Nelson..

Maxwell, John C. 2010. *Everyone Communicates, Few Connect: What the Most Effective People Do Differently.* Nashville, TN: Thomas Nelson.

Mehmood, Talat. "Bridging the Gap: Change in Class Environment to Help Learners Lower Affective Filters." *Arab World English Journal* 9, no. 3 (September 2018): 129-44. https://dx.doi.org/10.24093/awej/vol9no3.9.

Mehrabian, Albert. 1971. *Silent Messages.* Belmont, CA: Wadsworth Publishing Company.

Niles, Andrea N., Laurie J. Burklund, Jessica J. Arch, Matthew D. Lieberman, and Michelle G. Craske. 2018. "The Effects of Mindfulness on Negative Affect: A Neuroimaging Study." *Psychological Science* 29 (2): 250–259. https://doi.org/10.1177/0956797617739589.

Pianta, Robert C. 2006. "Classroom Management and Student-Teacher Relationships: Implications for Research and Practice." In *Handbook of Classroom Management: Research, Practice, and Contemporary Issues*, edited by C. M. Evertson and C. S. Weinstein, 3–20. Mahwah, NJ: Lawrence Erlbaum Associates.

Pennebaker, James W., and Joshua M. Smyth. 2016. *Opening Up by Writing It Down: How Expressive Writing Improves Health and Eases Emotional Pain.* 2nd ed. New York: The Guilford Press.

Porges, Stephen W. 2011. *The Polyvagal Theory: Neurophysiological Foundations of Emotions, Attachment, Communication, and Self-Regulation.* New York: Norton.

Rogers, Carl R. 1961. *On Becoming a Person: A Therapist's View of Psychotherapy.* Boston: Houghton Mifflin.

Rosenthal, Robert, and Lenore Jacobson. 1968. *Pygmalion in the Classroom: Teacher Expectation and Pupils' Intellectual Development.* New York: Holt, Rinehart & Winston.

Seligman, Martin E. P. 2011. *Flourish: A Visionary New Understanding of Happiness and Well-Being.* New York: Atria Books.

Schonert-Reichl, Kimberly A., Eva Oberle, Molly S. Lawlor, Donna Abbott, Kate Thomson, Theo F. Oberlander, and Adele Diamond. 2015. "Enhancing Cognitive and Social-Emotional Development Through a Simple-to-Administer Mindfulness-Based School Program for Elementary School Children: A Randomized Controlled Trial." *Developmental Psychology* 51 (1): 52–66. https://doi.org/10.1037/a0038454.

Schultz, Wolfram. 2015. "Dopamine Reward Prediction Error Coding." *Dialogues in Clinical Neuroscience* 17 (1): 23–32.

Sparby, Terje. 2018. "Gratitude Journaling and Its Impact on Psychological Well-Being: A Review of Empirical Studies." *The Journal of Positive Psychology* 13 (4): [page numbers needed].352-365. https://doi.org/10.1080/17439760.2018.1454455.

Spilt, Jantine L., Helma M. Koomen, and J. T. Thijs. "Teacher Well-Being: The Importance of Teacher–Student Relationships." *Educational Psychology Review* 23, no. 4 (2011): 457–77. https://doi.org/10.1007/s10648-011-9170-y.

Snyder, C. R. (1991). *Handbook of Hope: Theory, Measures, and Applications.* Academic Press.

Snyder, C. R. 2002. "Hope Theory: Rainbows in the Mind." *Psychological Inquiry* 13 (4): 249–275. https://doi.org/10.1207/S15327965PLI1304_01.

Snyder, C. R., Jennifer S. Cheavens, David B. Feldman, A. Gum, and Shane T. Michael. 2005. "Hope Therapy in a Community Sample: A Pilot Investigation." *Social Indicators Research* 77 (1): 61–78. https://doi.org/10.1007/s11205-005-5553-0.

Spilt, Jantine L., Helma M. Y. Koomen, and Jochem T. Thijs. 2011. "Teacher Well-Being: The Importance of Teacher–Student Relationships." *Educational Psychology Review* 23 (4): 457–477. https://doi.org/10.1007/s10648-011-9170-y.

Taylor, Shelley E. 2011. *Social Support: A Review of Psychological and Biological Processes.* New York: Oxford University Press.

Waldinger, Robert J., and Marc S. Schulz. 2023. *The Good Life: Lessons from the World's Longest Scientific Study of Happiness.* New York: Simon & Schuster.

Walton, Gregory M., and Geoffrey L. Cohen. 2011. "A Brief Social-Belonging Intervention Improves Academic and Health Outcomes of Minority Students." *Science* 331 (6023): 1447–1451. https://doi.org/10.1126/science.1198364.

Yap, L. A., C. Dillon, and K. S. Chew. 2022. "The Impact of Nature Imagery and Mystery on Attention Restoration." *Environmental Psychology Journal* 45 (2): 129–142. https://doi.org/10.1016/j.jenvp.2022.10192.

Yap, Alexander J., Susan T. Fiske, and Daniel M. Wegner. 2022. "Cognitive Reframing and the Impact of Visual Cues on Mental Resetting." *Journal of Applied Cognitive Psychology* 36 (2): 145–162. https://doi.org/10.1002/acp.3956.

Zak, Paul J. 2012. *The Moral Molecule: The Source of Love and Prosperity.* New York: Dutton.

Zerach, Gadi, Zahava Solomon, and R. J. Heruti. 2020. "PTSD, Distress, and Anxiety: Examining the Effectiveness of Grounding Techniques." *Journal of Anxiety Disorders* 74: 102266. https://doi.org/10.1016/j.janxdis.2020.102266.

About the Authors

Donita Grissom, Ph.D.

Dr. Donita Grissom's journey in education is a testament to her passion for teaching, empowering others, and fostering meaningful connections. Her path has been marked by dedication, expertise, and an unwavering commitment to equipping educators with the skills and knowledge to transform lives. With degrees from Southeast Missouri State University, the University of Florida, and a Ph.D. in TESOL from the University of Central Florida, Donita has shaped the field of multilingual education and teacher training, mentoring future leaders as the Ed.D. TESOL Specialization Advisor. Her research on Snyder's hope theory influenced a desire to support English learners facing trauma and has made her a sought-after keynote speaker, hope specialist, and life coach. As an English Specialist for the US State Department, she champions global collaboration, bridging cultures through language and education. Beyond academia, she is a mentor, professional consultant, and devoted mother and grandmother, embodying the true essence of an educator—one who not only imparts knowledge but also inspires hope, resilience, and transformation in others.

If you're looking for an inspiring keynote speaker, a dynamic professional development workshop, or expert coaching and mentoring for your team, Dr. Donita Grissom brings a wealth of knowledge, passion, and real-world experience to the Best Quester's team. As a specialist in multilingual education, teacher training, and hope theory, she empowers educators, leaders, and organizations with practical strategies to foster raising hope levels, reduce stress, increase resilience, and overall thriving in well-being. The Best Questers team delivers impactful sessions tailored to your needs.

Viki Kelchner, Ph.D.

Dr. Viki Kelchner is a globally recognized expert in counseling and education, known for her dedication to mental health wellness, trauma-informed care, and community-based interventions. As a licensed professional counselor, licensed professional supervisor, National Board-Certified counselor, and certified school counselor, she brings over 25 years of experience working with K–12 schools, educators, and families to improve outcomes for youth. Her research and publications focus on supporting individuals with neurodiversity, school-based family interventions, and fostering resilience in high-needs communities. She is passionate about forming partnerships that promote mental health literacy, trauma-responsive practices, and inclusive educational environments. As a counselor educator, she trains and supervises counselors-in-training to work with schools, families, and behavioral health organizations, ensuring a holistic approach to well-being. Beyond academia, she is a sought-after speaker, consultant, and curriculum developer. Deeply committed to making a lasting impact, Dr. Kelchner pours her heart into every initiative, believing that every step she takes brings her closer to creating a more compassionate and supportive world for all.

If you're looking for an inspiring keynote speaker, a dynamic professional development workshop, or expert coaching and mentoring for your team, Dr. Viki Kelchner brings a wealth of knowledge, passion, and real-world experience to the Best Questers team. As a specialist in mental health wellness, trauma-informed practices, community-based interventions, neurodivergence, and school-based family services, she is dedicated to equipping educators, leaders, and professionals with the tools to support youth and families effectively. Dr. Kelchner offers engaging workshops on trauma-responsive teaching, fostering mental health resilience in schools, neurodiversity-inclusive practices, and building strong school-community partnerships. The Best Questers team delivers impactful, customized sessions tailored to your organization's needs.

Debbie Simões, M.Ed.

A unique ability to see potential beyond circumstances enables Debbie to turn stumbling blocks into stepping stones, empowering educators to bridge the gap between potential and performance. Inspired by a college professor who introduced her to leaders such as Zig Ziglar and John Maxwell, she knew early on that teaching and inspiring others was her calling. Despite a brain injury that prevented her from completing student teaching as an undergrad, she went on to earn an MEd from Arizona State University and another from the University of Maryland.

As an educator in Phoenix, Washington, DC, and South Florida, Debbie saw firsthand the urgent need to equip educators with the skills to cultivate vibrant, connected learning communities where happiness and high achievement are an everyday reality. She's navigated the complexities of education as a teacher, principal, and director of a university lab school, equipping her with the insights to empower young scholars and educators at every level. She is a Nationally Certified Trainer with the Center for Teacher Effectiveness, a Maxwell Leadership Certified Speaker, Trainer, and Coach, and a certified life and business coach with a heart to add value to others. In 2021, she founded Best Questers to skyrocket teacher retention and student achievement through dynamic, data-backed professional development that helps teachers and students love stepping into their greatness together every day. When she's not out Best-Questing, Debbie enjoys her South Florida garden sanctuary with Mr. Fabulous (her husband), their yellow lab, Buddy, and the fab four felines.

Are you ready to say yes to the practical, outside-the-box solutions you've been missing—higher teacher retention, student attendance, motivation, achievement? Say no to the same old struggles, costly curriculums, and band-aid fixes that don't move the needle.

Debbie is available to provide professional development to help build the future your school or district deserves! Available for get-up-and-go keynotes, retreats, professional learning, team building, group coaching and community building! She offers "Time to Teach Classroom Leadership Workshops" to deliver proactive strategies to predict and prevent problem behaviors, maintain self-control, and preserve the integrity of instruction (available for college credit).

To schedule an event or discuss collaboration opportunities,
contact **info@bestquesters.net.**

Bring High Five to Thrive into Your School or District

The Problem

So many educators are feeling overburdened and undervalued—losing hope that they can still make the difference they were called to make. Stress and burnout have made teacher retention an urgent, nationwide challenge.

The Solution

High Five to Thrive offers five simple, practical strategies to help educators manage stress, create calm and connected classrooms, and rediscover the joy of teaching. These powerful practices restore hope and equip educators to operate at their full potential—empowered, energized, and excited to show up each day—so students and school communities can thrive with them

Empowering Educators. Transforming Classrooms. One Quest at a Time

At Best Questers, we specialize in delivering top-tier professional learning and educational solutions designed for teachers, school leaders, support staff, and students. Whether you're an educator seeking to elevate your practice or a school aiming to strengthen student success, our tailored programs provide the knowledge, tools, and strategies to help every learner thrive. Committed to empowering educators and transforming classrooms, Best Questers turns training into transformation—one quest at a time.

Best Questers offer expert-led workshops, training, and consulting services designed to empower educators, caregivers, students, and corporate professionals. Our programs provide strategic insights and hands-on learning experiences that drive success in both academic and professional settings. Whether you're an educator looking to enhance instructional methods, a caregiver seeking specialized training, a student preparing for career advancement, or a business aiming to improve workforce skills, our tailored solutions ensure impactful learning and growth.

Bring energy and purpose to your next event with impactful keynote presentations and interactive speaking engagements designed to inspire, educate, and empower. Our signature sessions include *"High Five to Thrive: Five Proven Practices to Unleash Your Passion for Teaching,"* a powerful framework for boosting educator wellness, student achievement, and school culture, and *"The BOOST Playbook: How to Engage and Support Multilingual Learners in Any Classroom,"* which equips educators with practical strategies for multilingual student language and academic success.

Additional topics cover hopeful leadership; trauma-informed teaching; student wellbeing and whole child thriving; positive changes by raising hope levels; mental health wellness/mental health literacy; how to manage stress; self compassion; self-care; healthy connections and boundaries; culturally responsive instruction; and more.. Whether you're planning a conference, district PD day, corporate training, or community event, we tailor each presentation to meet the unique needs of your audience—delivering research-based, story-driven content that fosters growth and transformation. Now booking for organizations seeking engaging, relatable, and results-oriented speakers. To schedule an event or discuss collaboration opportunities, contact info@bestquesters.net.

Other Books by Best Questers

The BOOST Playbook: How to Engage and Support Multilingual Learners in Any Classroom is a practical, research-based guide that helps teachers support multilingual learners with five powerful "BOOST Moves." These moves—visual scaffolds, targeted vocabulary, structured interaction, clear teacher talk, and academic discourse—equip educators to break down language barriers and boost student engagement and achievement. Packed with real classroom examples, planning tools, and ready-to-use strategies, *The BOOST Playbook* offers solutions for making lessons more accessible, inclusive, and effective for all learners.

Custom Learning Solutions

We understand that one size does not fit all when it comes to education and professional training. Our customized learning solutions are designed to meet the unique needs of institutions, businesses, and individuals. From tailored corporate training programs to private coaching sessions, we craft personalized strategies that align with specific goals and challenges. Whether you're looking for institution-wide training or one-on-one professional development, we provide specialized support to help you succeed.

What People Are Saying

"Thank you so much for your dedication and commitment to the VIQI Project! Your partnership has been instrumental and we couldn't have done this without you. Thank you for navigating your challenges so gracefully and for your unwavering support to the teachers and children of St. Lucie."

—**Isabel Acosta,** Variations in Implementation of Quality Interventions (VIQI): Examining the Quality Child Outcomes Relationship in Child Care and Early Education

"Thank you so much for the time and attention you dedicated to provide sessions specifically tailored to build on our professional learning plan and for including every detail we discussed. Your attention to our district needs went above and beyond expectations. I'm very grateful for the feedback you were able to provide based on session discussions. It will serve to guide our next steps and follow up with administration."

—**Tracie Carollo,** Secondary ELA Specialist/World Languages, Escambia County Public Schools

www.ingramcontent.com/pod-product-compliance
Lightning Source LLC
Chambersburg PA
CBHW080958120626
46546CB00010B/2955